MathFlare

Name: ________________________

Class: ___________

Teacher: ________________________

Introduction

As parents and educators, we recognize the pivotal role mathematics plays in shaping a child's academic journey and future success. Yet, the path to mathematical proficiency can often seem daunting, fraught with challenges and complexities. That's where the transformative power of MathFlare Workbooks shine through, illuminating the way forward with clarity, precision, and purpose.

Introducing MathFlare Workbooks – a beacon of guidance, a testament to excellence, and a catalyst for achievement. Crafted with meticulous care and expertise, MathFlare Workbooks stand as paragons of educational excellence, designed to nurture young minds, ignite a passion for learning, and develop a deep-rooted understanding of mathematical concepts.

Picture this: your child eagerly delves into the pages of Mathflare Workbook, greeted by a step-by-step guide illuminated with vivid examples that demystify complex mathematical concepts. With each turn of the page, they embark on a journey of discovery, encountering thoughtfully curated practice questions that reinforce learning and hone problem-solving skills. And when they unveil the answers to those very questions, a sense of accomplishment blossoms within them – a tangible reward for their hard work and dedication.

But MathFlare Workbooks are more than just tools for learning; they are pathways to comprehension, fostering a deep-seated understanding of mathematical concepts through a sequential, logical flow. From fundamental principles to advanced problem-solving strategies, every chapter builds upon the last, ensuring a robust foundation upon which future knowledge can be constructed.

As parents, we yearn for nothing more than to see our children thrive, to witness the spark of inspiration ignited within them as they conquer academic challenges with confidence and poise. MathFlare Workbooks serve as partners in this noble endeavor, offering not just practice questions, but the keys to unlocking a world of opportunity.

And for teachers, MathFlare Workbooks stand as invaluable allies in the quest to cultivate mathematical proficiency in the classroom. With answers readily available, instructors can focus on guiding and nurturing their students, confident in the knowledge that MathFlare Workbooks provide a solid framework upon which to build.

In the pages of MathFlare Workbooks, we find not just the promise of academic excellence, but the seeds of a brighter tomorrow. So let us embrace the power of mathematics, let us champion the journey of learning, and let us pave the way for a generation of young minds poised to shape the world. With MathFlare Workbooks as our guide, the possibilities are infinite, and the future, bright.

Table of Contents

Addition and Subtraction	
Addition with Regrouping	1
Subtraction with Regrouping	9
Addition: Unknown Numbers	17
Subtraction: Unknown Numbers	23
Make 1000	29
Addition: 3 Addends	32
Multiple Operations: Addition Subtraction	44

MathFlare
2
MATH
WORKBOOK
Step by Step Guide
and Essential Practice
with Answers
Addition
Subtraction
Multiplication
Place Value and
Expanded
Notations
Geometry
MathFlare Publishing

MathFlare
2-3
MATH
WORKBOOK
Step by Step Guide
and Essential Practice
with Answers
Addition
Subtraction
Multiplication
and Division
Place Value and
Expanded
Notations
Geometry
MathFlare Publishing

MathFlare
3
MATH
WORKBOOK
Step by Step Guide
and Essential Practice
with Answers
Multiplication
and Division
Decimals
Place Value and
Expanded
Notations
Fractions
and Geometry

MathFlare
1
MATH
WORKBOOK
Step by Step Guide
and Essential Practice
with Answers
Counting and
Numbers
Addition and
Subtraction
Place Value and
Expanded
Notations
Understanding
Time
MathFlare Publishing

MathFlare
1-2
MATH
WORKBOOK
Step by Step Guide
and Essential Practice
with Answers
Counting and
Numbers
Addition and
Subtraction
Place Value and
Expanded
Notations
Understanding
Time
MathFlare Publishing

MathFlare
3-4
MATH
WORKBOOK
Step by Step Guide
and Essential Practice
with Answers
Addition
Subtraction
Multiplication
Division
Place Value and
Expanded
Notations
Fractions
and Geometry
MathFlare Publishing

MathFlare
4
MATH
WORKBOOK
Step by Step Guide
and Essential Practice
with Answers
Addition
Subtraction
Multiplication
Division
Place Value and
Expanded
Notations
Fractions
and Geometry
MathFlare Publishing

MathFlare
4-5
MATH
WORKBOOK
Step by Step Guide
and Essential Practice
with Answers
Multiplication
Division
Place Value and
Expanded
Notations
Fractions
and Geometry
Unit
Conversion
MathFlare Publishing

MathFlare
Grade 5
MATH WORKBOOK
Step by Step Guide and Essential Practice with Answers
Multiplication Division
Place Value and Expanded Notations
Fractions and Geometry
Unit Conversion
MathFlare Publishing

MathFlare
Grade 5-6
MATH WORKBOOK
Step by Step Guide and Essential Practice with Answers
Multiplication Division
Place Value and Expanded Notations
Fractions and Geometry
Units and Statistics
MathFlare Publishing

MathFlare
Grade 6
MATH WORKBOOK
Step by Step Guide and Essential Practice with Answers
Integers and Statistics
Arithmetic and Pre-Algebra
Fractions and Geometry
Ratio and Percentage
MathFlare Publishing

MathFlare
Grade 6-7
MATH WORKBOOK
Step by Step Guide and Essential Practice with Answers
Arithmetic and Pre-Algebra
Ratio, Percent Proportion
Geometry
Statistics
MathFlare Publishing

MathFlare
Grade 7
MATH WORKBOOK
Step by Step Guide and Essential Practice with Answers
Pre-Algebra
Ratio, Percent Proportion
Geometry
Statistics
MathFlare Publishing

MathFlare
Grade 7-8
MATH WORKBOOK
Step by Step Guide and Essential Practice with Answers
Pre-Algebra
Ratio, Percent Proportion
Geometry and Cartesian Plane
Statistics
MathFlare Publishing

MathFlare
Grade 8-9
MATH WORKBOOK
Step by Step Guide and Essential Practice with Answers
Pre-Algebra
Ratio, Proportion and Percentage
Linear Equations
Geometry and Cartesian Plane
MathFlare Publishing

MathFlare
Grade 8
MATH WORKBOOK
Step by Step Guide and Essential Practice with Answers
Pre-Algebra
Percentage
Linear Equations
Geometry
MathFlare Publishing

Addition and Subtraction

Addition with Regrouping

When we do addition, we combine numbers. But sometimes, when we're adding numbers, we might need to regroup. Regrouping means we have to move a number from one place to another, usually to the next column, to get the right answer.

For Example: Let's take an example of adding 533 and 579 together:

$$\begin{array}{r} 5\ 3\ 3 \\ +\ 5\ 7\ 9 \\ \hline \end{array}$$

First, we start by adding the digits in the ones place: 3 + 9 = 12. We write down the 2 in the ones place and carry over the 1 to the tens place.

$$\begin{array}{r} 1 \\ 5\ 3\ 3 \\ +\ 5\ 7\ 9 \\ \hline 2 \end{array}$$

Now, we add the digits in the tens place, along with the carry-over: 2 + 8 + 1 = 11. We write down the 1 in the tens place and carry over the 1 to the hundreds place.

$$\begin{array}{r} 1\ 1 \\ 5\ 2\ 2 \\ +\ 5\ 8\ 9 \\ \hline 1\ 2 \end{array}$$

Now, we add the digits in the hundreds place, along with the carry-over: 5 + 5 + 1 = 11. We write down the 1 in the tens place and carry over the 1 to the hundreds place.

$$
\begin{array}{r}
1\ 1 \\
5\ 2\ 2 \\
+\ 5\ 8\ 9 \\
\hline
1\ 1\ 1\ 2
\end{array}
$$

This process of carrying over helps us accurately add numbers, especially when they're larger.

Subtraction with Regrouping

Subtraction is a key math operation where we find the difference between two numbers. Sometimes, when we subtract, we might need to regroup, which means borrowing from the next column.

Let's take an example of subtracting 436 from 563:

First, we start by subtracting the digits in the ones place: 3 - 6.

Since 3 is less than 6, we need to regroup. We borrow 1 from the tens place, making it 5 tens instead of 6, and add it to the ones place.

So, 3 becomes 13, and then we subtract 6.

$$
\begin{array}{r}
5\ \ 6\ 13 \\
-\ 4\ \ 3\ \ 6 \\
\hline
7
\end{array}
$$

Now, we subtract the tens place digits: 5 - 3 = 2

$$
\begin{array}{r}
5 \\
5\ \ \cancel{6}\,13 \\
-\ 4\ 3\ 6 \\
\hline
2\ 7
\end{array}
$$

Now, we subtract the hundreds place digits: 5 - 4 = 1

$$5$$

$$5\ \cancel{6}\,13$$

$$-\ 4\ 3\ 6$$

$$1\ 2\ 7$$

This process of regrouping or borrowing helps us accurately subtract numbers, especially when the top digit is smaller than the bottom one.

Let's solve problems from exercises:

$$
\begin{array}{r} 714 \\ +\ 797 \\ \hline 1{,}511 \end{array}
\qquad
\begin{array}{r} 980 \\ -\ 896 \\ \hline 84 \end{array}
$$

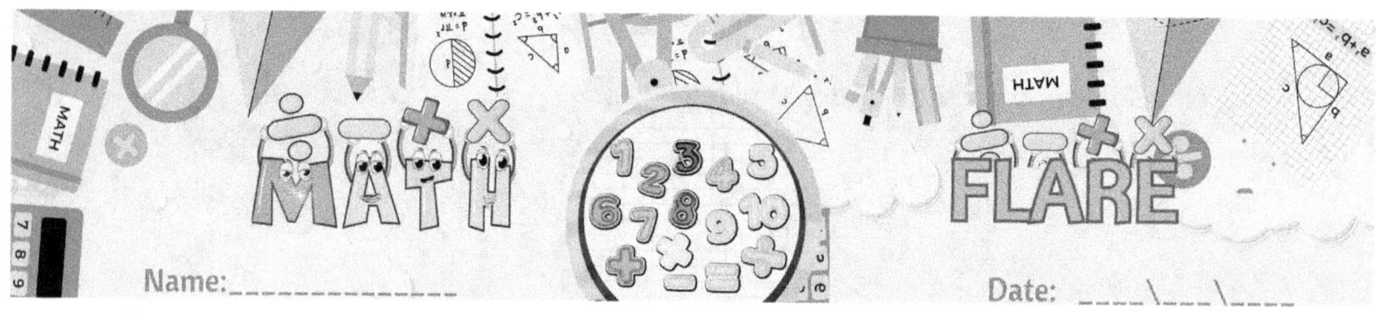

Addition with Regrouping

Find the sum.

1. 853 + 798	2. 488 + 855	3. 921 + 389	4. 819 + 792
5. 851 + 979	6. 161 + 949	7. 737 + 794	8. 171 + 949
9. 558 + 569	10. 655 + 586	11. 977 + 983	12. 586 + 658
13. 578 + 798	14. 414 + 698	15. 761 + 689	16. 454 + 659

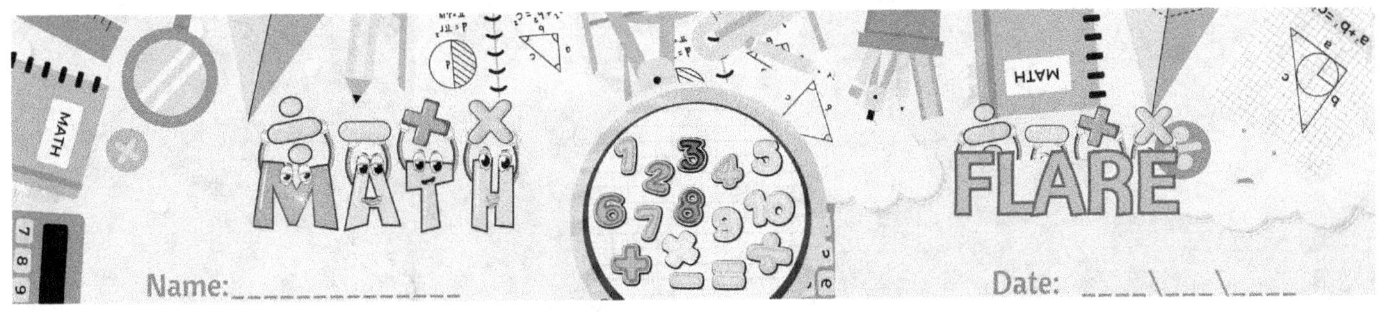

17. 274 + 936	18. 428 + 997	19. 292 + 838	20. 996 + 965
21. 664 + 786	22. 749 + 961	23. 684 + 447	24. 436 + 685
25. 568 + 945	26. 629 + 881	27. 753 + 477	28. 871 + 869
29. 311 + 799	30. 776 + 799	31. 928 + 395	32. 971 + 379
33. 547 + 583	34. 371 + 969	35. 695 + 717	36. 827 + 586

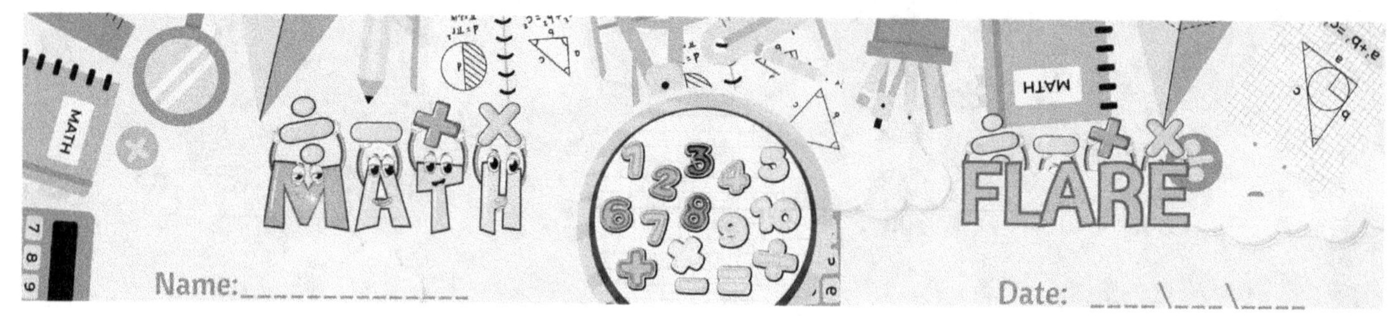

<table>
<tr><td>37.
572
+ 698</td><td>38.
651
+ 899</td><td>39.
334
+ 878</td><td>40.
433
+ 977</td></tr>
<tr><td>41.
784
+ 388</td><td>42.
949
+ 775</td><td>43.
119
+ 993</td><td>44.
355
+ 879</td></tr>
<tr><td>45.
761
+ 559</td><td>46.
246
+ 875</td><td>47.
324
+ 897</td><td>48.
134
+ 976</td></tr>
<tr><td>49.
815
+ 595</td><td>50.
514
+ 698</td><td>51.
936
+ 376</td><td>52.
489
+ 853</td></tr>
<tr><td>53.
317
+ 993</td><td>54.
648
+ 662</td><td>55.
819
+ 694</td><td>56.
635
+ 685</td></tr>
</table>

57. 138 + 985	58. 115 + 996	59. 441 + 969	60. 315 + 795
61. 796 + 567	62. 445 + 968	63. 567 + 876	64. 331 + 979
65. 657 + 878	66. 475 + 798	67. 211 + 899	68. 434 + 979
69. 828 + 696	70. 498 + 935	71. 684 + 897	72. 982 + 179
73. 921 + 589	74. 783 + 848	75. 282 + 928	76. 931 + 589

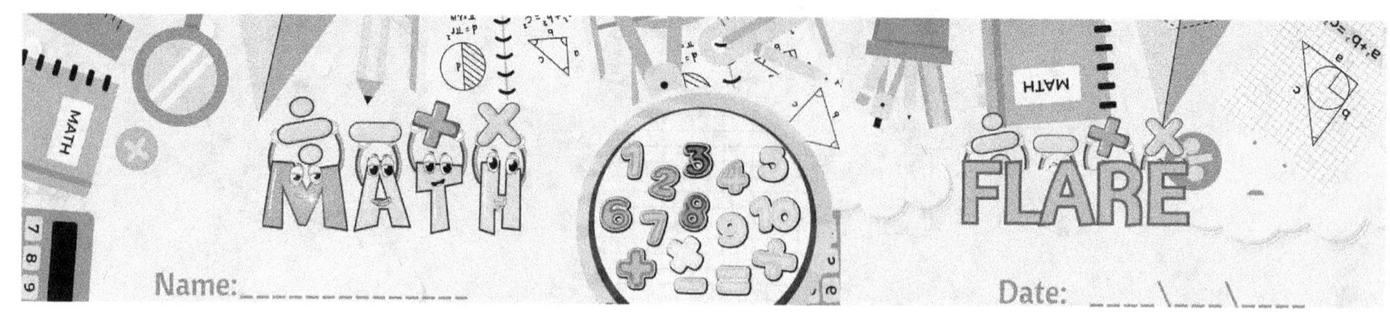

77. 331 + 799	78. 835 + 477	79. 885 + 357	80. 386 + 738
81. 841 + 379	82. 513 + 598	83. 316 + 896	84. 575 + 637
85. 171 + 969	86. 881 + 349	87. 857 + 369	88. 631 + 699
89. 583 + 867	90. 316 + 998	91. 322 + 898	92. 193 + 937
93. 447 + 995	94. 568 + 965	95. 964 + 966	96. 667 + 577

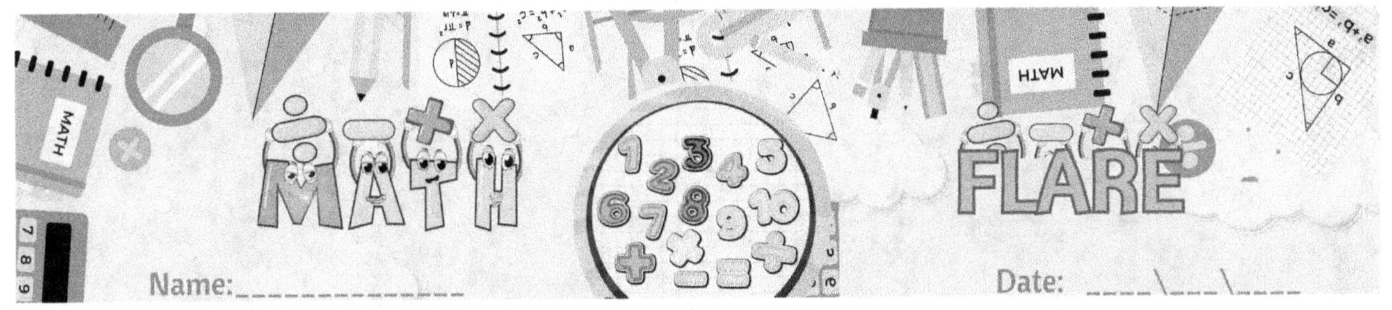

97. 819 + 297	98. 195 + 915	99. 789 + 542	100. 873 + 887
101. 984 + 546	102. 747 + 793	103. 542 + 688	104. 711 + 999
105. 668 + 462	106. 886 + 624	107. 135 + 978	108. 988 + 428
109. 279 + 971	110. 194 + 997	111. 368 + 763	112. 373 + 799
113. 893 + 498	114. 536 + 674	115. 274 + 859	116. 813 + 399

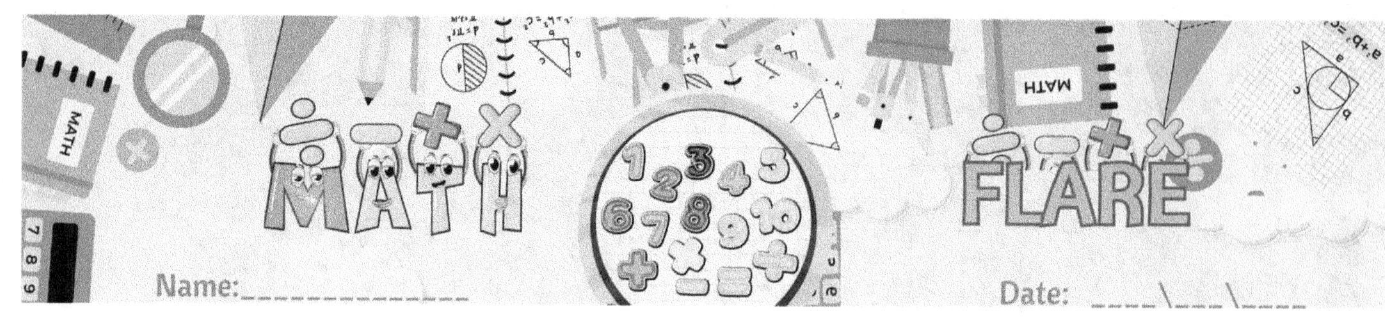

117. 491 + 939	118. 122 + 988	119. 764 + 478	120. 791 + 769
121. 314 + 796	122. 342 + 779	123. 178 + 947	124. 542 + 568
125. 298 + 965	126. 232 + 879	127. 448 + 783	128. 816 + 495
129. 273 + 847	130. 827 + 299	131. 248 + 862	132. 787 + 459
133. 518 + 894	134. 229 + 993	135. 356 + 984	136. 664 + 856

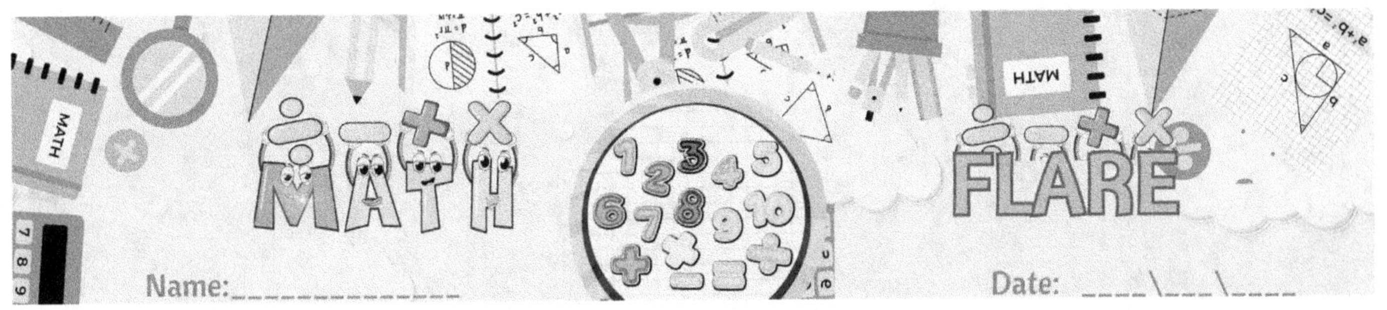

137. 478 + 736	138. 176 + 967	139. 421 + 699	140. 128 + 986
141. 861 + 389	142. 472 + 858	143. 186 + 997	144. 692 + 949
145. 413 + 797	146. 611 + 999	147. 644 + 686	148. 613 + 898
149. 818 + 892	150. 917 + 698	151. 274 + 987	152. 212 + 998
153. 242 + 979	154. 518 + 795	155. 111 + 999	156. 612 + 998

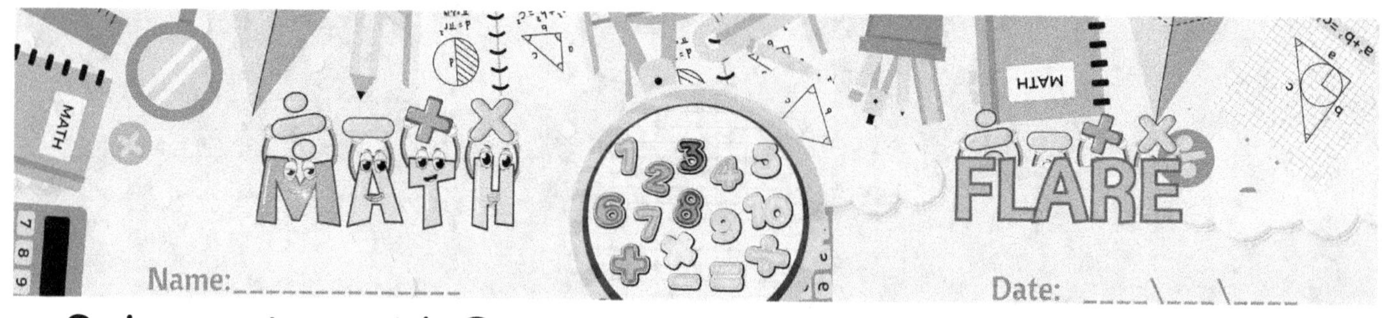

Subtraction with Regrouping

Find the difference.

157.
886
- 797

158.
542
- 354

159.
606
- 419

160.
723
- 454

161.
918
- 849

162.
782
- 499

163.
824
- 657

164.
788
- 399

165.
385
- 296

166.
380
- 299

167.
212
- 196

168.
538
- 499

169.
858
- 299

170.
384
- 195

171.
971
- 287

172.
210
- 189

173. 658 − 469	174. 225 − 147	175. 202 − 127	176. 500 − 361
177. 624 − 265	178. 461 − 188	179. 476 − 289	180. 612 − 147
181. 222 − 177	182. 911 − 688	183. 524 − 346	184. 958 − 489
185. 633 − 485	186. 445 − 278	187. 688 − 499	188. 888 − 799

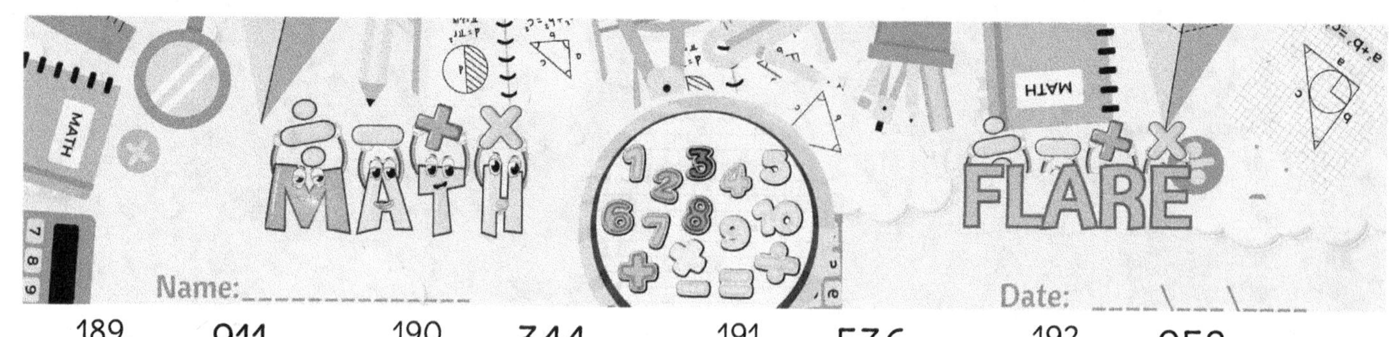

189. 911 − 842	190. 344 − 255	191. 536 − 248	192. 952 − 493
193. 385 − 297	194. 487 − 298	195. 278 − 189	196. 581 − 499
197. 871 − 795	198. 848 − 179	199. 288 − 199	200. 234 − 198
201. 266 − 179	202. 568 − 379	203. 255 − 198	204. 987 − 898

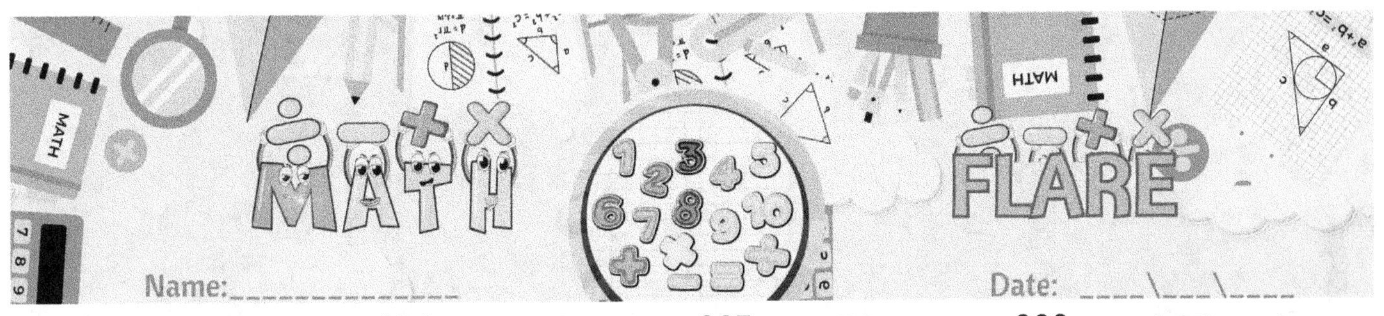

205.   581
   - 398
	206. 406
	   - 269
		207. 381
		   - 292
			208. 646
			   - 557

209.   276
   - 198
	210. 568
	   - 399
		211. 272
		   - 183
			212. 521
			   - 445

213.   368
   - 289
	214. 588
	   - 499
		215. 783
		   - 698
			216. 804
			   - 648

217.   744
   - 157
	218. 683
	   - 498
		219. 808
		   - 389
			220. 458
			   - 289

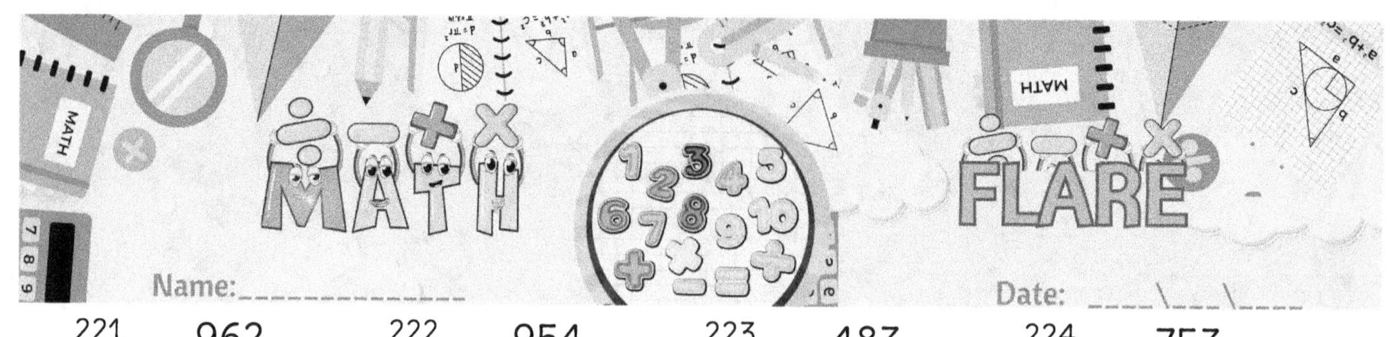

221. 962 − 479

222. 954 − 595

223. 483 − 396

224. 753 − 666

225. 405 − 147

226. 824 − 588

227. 648 − 469

228. 248 − 179

229. 541 − 357

230. 324 − 266

231. 226 − 137

232. 307 − 268

233. 753 − 477

234. 853 − 279

235. 360 − 275

236. 234 − 177

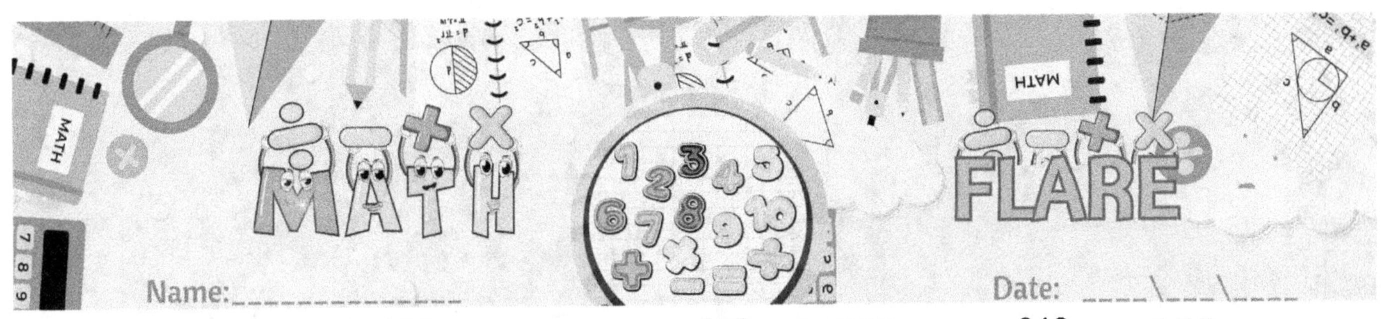

237. 240 - 156	238. 600 - 429	239. 557 - 489	240. 660 - 389
241. 956 - 669	242. 431 - 349	243. 961 - 279	244. 245 - 178
245. 975 - 199	246. 232 - 147	247. 336 - 289	248. 434 - 358
249. 866 - 678	250. 231 - 184	251. 757 - 368	252. 971 - 189

253. 658 − 499	254. 270 − 189	255. 286 − 198	256. 962 − 888
257. 587 − 399	258. 928 − 499	259. 842 − 556	260. 466 − 378
261. 282 − 194	262. 840 − 765	263. 678 − 189	264. 773 − 688
265. 487 − 299	266. 933 − 876	267. 453 − 286	268. 923 − 875

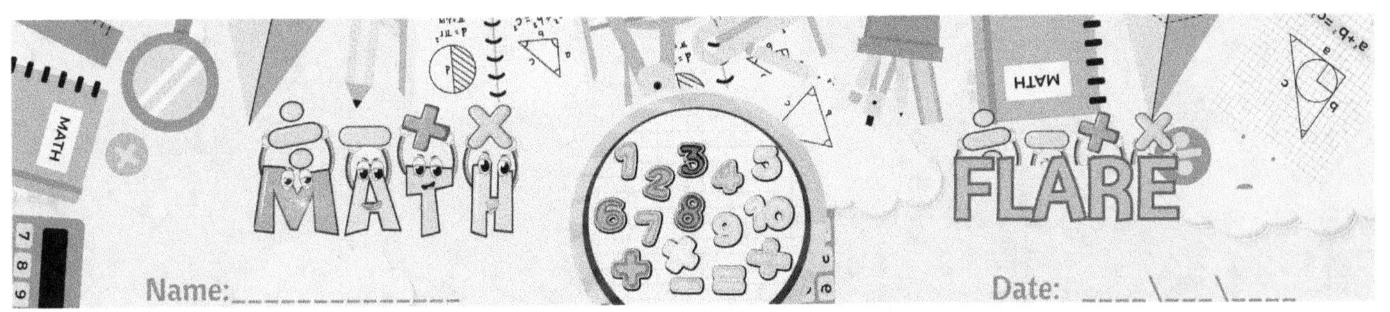

269. 805 − 768	270. 545 − 389	271. 204 − 175	272. 944 − 467
273. 322 − 173	274. 425 − 387	275. 772 − 598	276. 407 − 179
277. 406 − 187	278. 313 − 227	279. 581 − 197	280. 428 − 259
281. 966 − 299	282. 983 − 796	283. 805 − 159	284. 486 − 198

Addition Unknown Number

Find the unknown number.

285. 21 + 89 = _____

286. 15 + 98 = _____

287. 57 + 99 = _____

288. 7 + _____ = 60

289. _____ + 7 = 63

290. 12 + _____ = 111

291. 19 + 91 = _____

292. 48 + 93 = _____

293. 61 + _____ = 120

294. 22 + 89 = _____

295. _____ + 92 = 120

296. 47 + 79 = _____

297. 41 + 79 = _____

298. 62 + _____ = 70

299. 11 + _____ = 110

300. 81 + 29 = _____

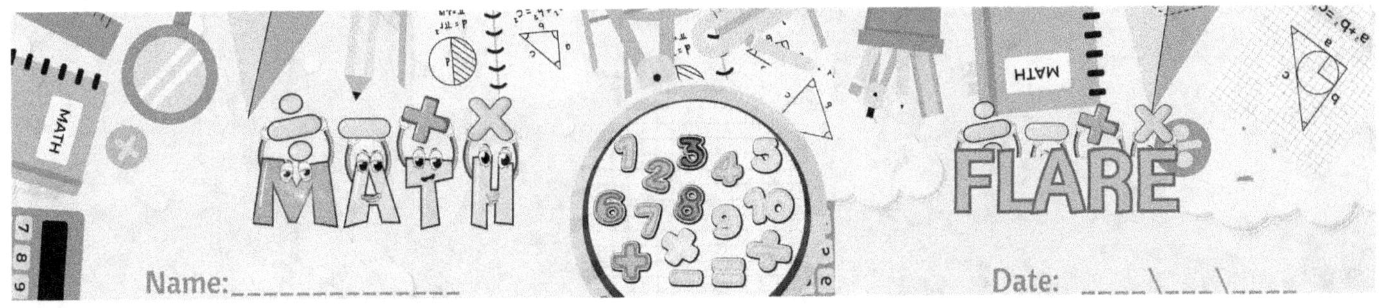

301. _____ + 78 = 171

302. _____ + 78 = 86

303. 58 + 79 = _____

304. 89 + _____ = 161

305. _____ + 8 = 40

306. 39 + 76 = _____

307. 14 + 98 = _____

308. _____ + 94 = 110

309. 34 + _____ = 133

310. 45 + 87 = _____

311. 43 + 97 = _____

312. 72 + 48 = _____

313. 13 + _____ = 112

314. 47 + _____ = 51

315. 43 + 8 = _____

316. _____ + 99 = 120

317. 77 + 46 = _____

318. 69 + _____ = 144

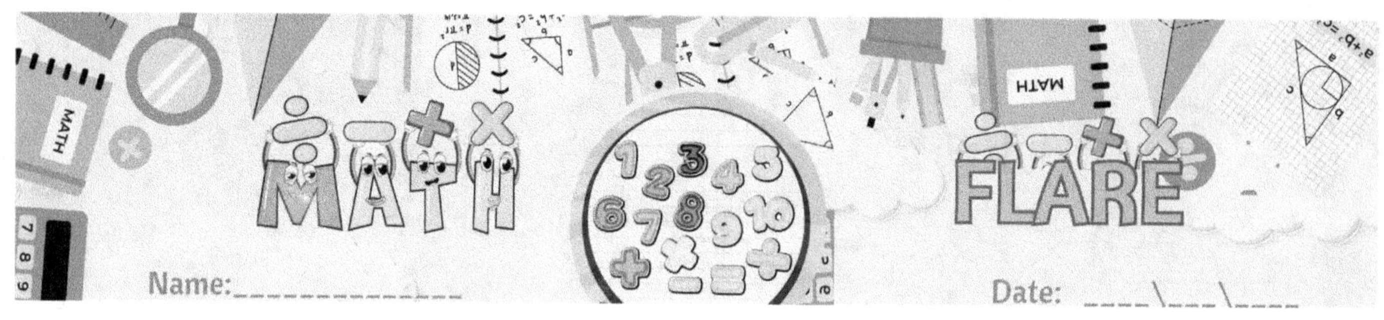

319. 86 + _____ = 173

320. 96 + 59 = _____

321. 89 + 55 = _____

322. 79 + _____ = 124

323. _____ + 89 = 123

324. 64 + _____ = 142

325. 88 + 56 = _____

326. _____ + 99 = 115

327. 74 + _____ = 81

328. 36 + 84 = _____

329. 1 + 69 = _____

330. _____ + 78 = 143

331. _____ + 88 = 113

332. 31 + _____ = 130

333. 81 + 49 = _____

334. _____ + 79 = 160

335. _____ + 58 = 125

336. _____ + 97 = 122

337. ____ + 86 = 183

338. ____ + 89 = 120

339. ____ + 98 = 110

340. 91 + 69 = ____

341. ____ + 93 = 111

342. 4 + ____ = 43

343. 74 + 39 = ____

344. 18 + ____ = 117

345. 27 + ____ = 34

346. ____ + 85 = 111

347. 64 + ____ = 150

348. ____ + 94 = 192

349. 54 + 69 = ____

350. ____ + 63 = 151

351. 35 + 85 = ____

352. 8 + ____ = 57

353. 3 + 79 = ____

354. 55 + ____ = 140

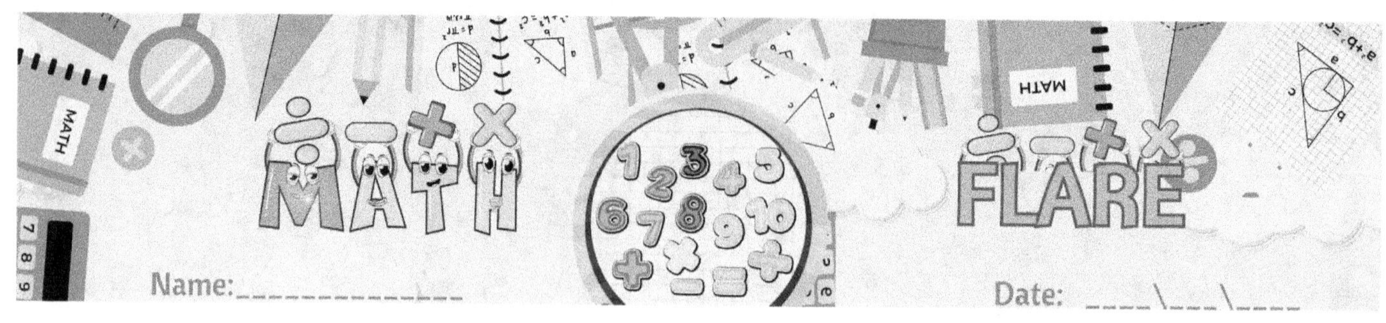

355. ____ + 57 = 120

356. 77 + ____ = 121

357. 33 + 89 = ____

358. ____ + 81 = 110

359. 71 + 89 = ____

360. 65 + 45 = ____

361. 34 + ____ = 41

362. ____ + 96 = 163

363. ____ + 79 = 140

364. ____ + 48 = 110

365. 33 + ____ = 131

366. 98 + ____ = 127

367. 26 + 98 = ____

368. 64 + ____ = 122

369. ____ + 3 = 40

370. 67 + 86 = ____

371. ____ + 75 = 130

372. 24 + 89 = ____

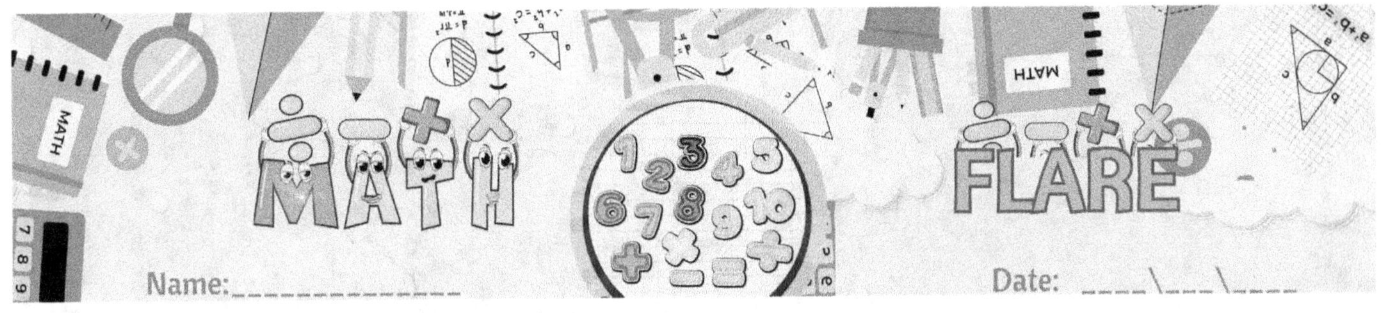

373. ____ + 98 = 121

374. 58 + 88 = ____

375. 82 + 49 = ____

376. ____ + 79 = 110

377. 14 + 99 = ____

378. 87 + ____ = 114

379. ____ + 39 = 42

380. 93 + ____ = 192

381. 46 + 76 = ____

382. 44 + ____ = 110

383. 78 + 58 = ____

384. 51 + 99 = ____

385. 73 + ____ = 150

386. 53 + 69 = ____

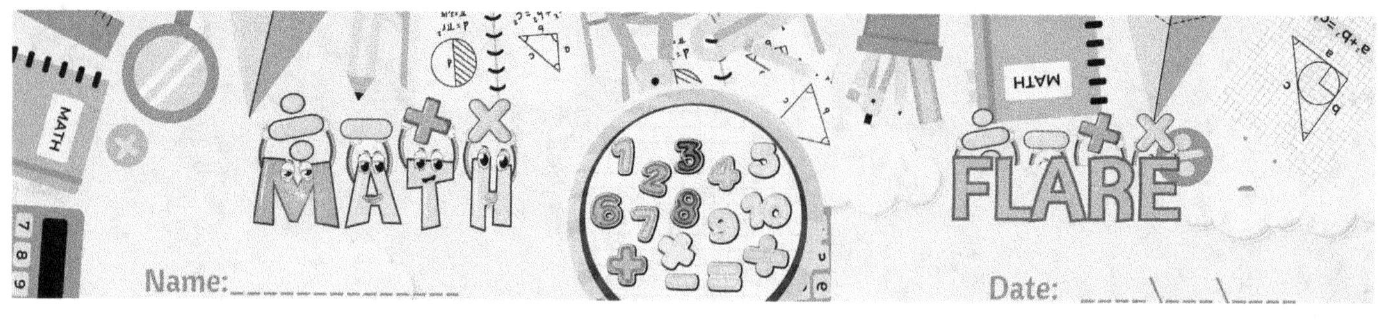

Subtraction: Unknown Number

Find the unknown number.

387. ___ − 34 = 12

388. ___ − 35 = 49

389. 28 − 23 = ___

390. 39 − 36 = ___

391. 76 − ___ = 62

392. 49 − ___ = 29

393. 28 − ___ = 11

394. ___ − 42 = 50

395. 30 − 21 = ___

396. 74 − ___ = 31

397. 11 − ___ = 1

398. 26 − ___ = 14

399. 92 − ___ = 51

400. ___ − 40 = 56

401. ___ − 33 = 66

402. ___ − 37 = 19

403. 79 - 17 = ___

404. 41 - 30 = ___

405. 91 - ___ = 19

406. ___ - 65 = 14

407. ___ - 26 = 0

408. 31 - 30 = ___

409. ___ - 45 = 14

410. 53 - 28 = ___

411. ___ - 11 = 67

412. ___ - 13 = 3

413. ___ - 80 = 9

414. ___ - 89 = 5

415. ___ - 40 = 14

416. 46 - ___ = 6

417. 77 - 76 = ___

418. 91 - ___ = 42

419. 58 - ___ = 7

420. ___ - 14 = 38

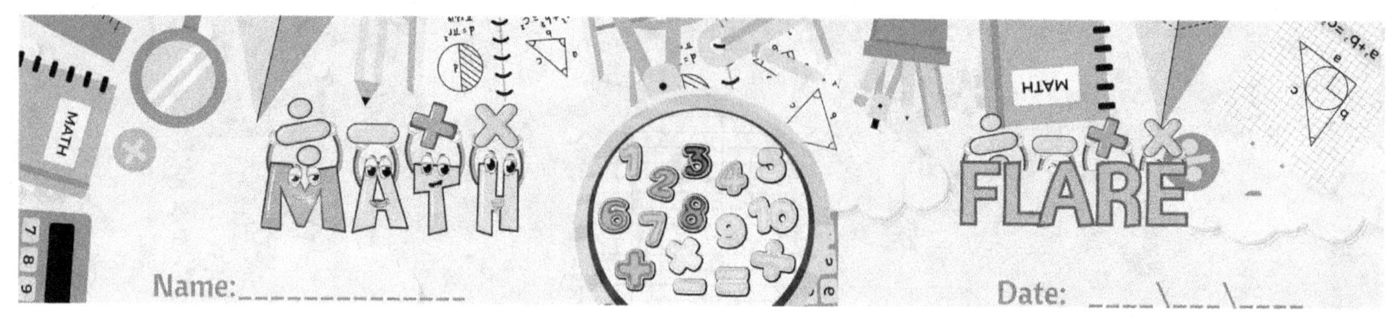

421. 14 - 11 = ___

422. ___ - 30 = 23

423. 79 - ___ = 6

424. ___ - 11 = 29

425. 30 - ___ = 15

426. 63 - ___ = 42

427. 89 - ___ = 35

428. ___ - 61 = 1

429. ___ - 12 = 15

430. 72 - ___ = 7

431. ___ - 16 = 9

432. ___ - 13 = 10

433. ___ - 39 = 2

434. 15 - ___ = 4

435. ___ - 15 = 2

436. ___ - 35 = 11

437. 31 - ___ = 13

438. ___ - 26 = 17

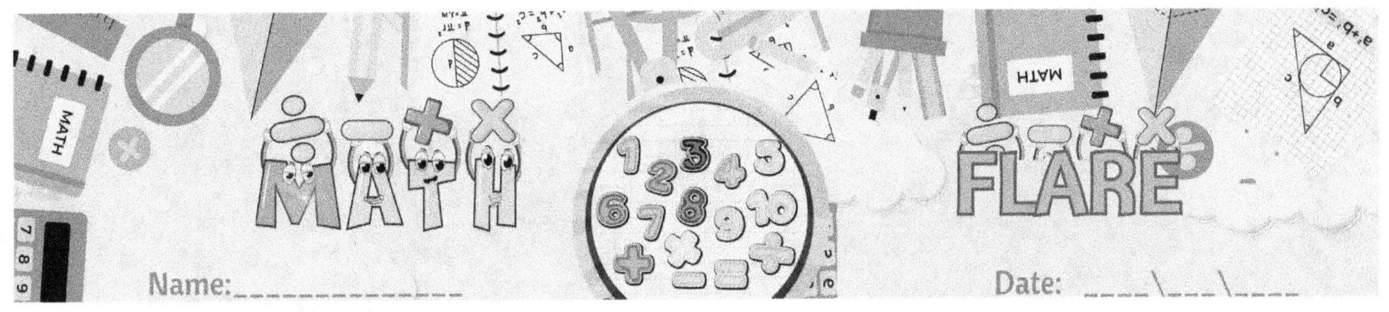

439. ___ - 38 = 19

440. ___ - 65 = 2

441. 59 - 55 = ___

442. 74 - ___ = 48

443. ___ - 12 = 6

444. ___ - 26 = 68

445. 46 - ___ = 3

446. 36 - ___ = 15

447. ___ - 18 = 5

448. 93 - ___ = 29

449. 20 - 18 = ___

450. ___ - 21 = 66

451. 94 - 50 = ___

452. ___ - 76 = 8

453. 97 - 53 = ___

454. ___ - 34 = 17

455. ___ - 39 = 11

456. ___ - 17 = 22

457. 71 - ___ = 6

458. 21 - ___ = 9

459. ___ - 10 = 0

460. 80 - 21 = ___

461. 51 - ___ = 1

462. 59 - 41 = ___

463. 51 - 40 = ___

464. 39 - ___ = 21

465. 54 - 46 = ___

466. ___ - 14 = 5

467. ___ - 31 = 67

468. 47 - 17 = ___

469. 29 - 18 = ___

470. ___ - 39 = 12

471. 98 - 47 = ___

472. 34 - ___ = 7

473. ___ - 31 = 64

474. ___ - 21 = 1

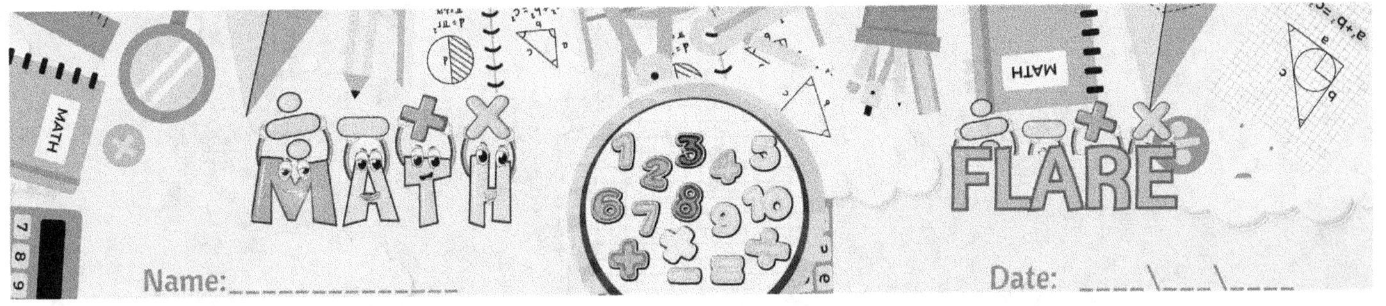

475. 84 - ___ = 73

476. 42 - ___ = 7

477. 11 - 11 = ___

478. 40 - ___ = 20

479. 13 - 11 = ___

480. ___ - 24 = 56

481. ___ - 15 = 3

482. ___ - 60 = 5

483. ___ - 20 = 12

484. 52 - 49 = ___

485. 94 - ___ = 37

486. 86 - 48 = ___

487. ___ - 57 = 15

488. 97 - 22 = ___

489. ___ - 36 = 8

490. ___ - 15 = 63

Name:_________________   Date: _______________

Make 1000

Add a number to the first number to make 1000.

491. 539 + ____ = 1,000   492. 97 + ____ = 1,000

493. 203 + ____ = 1,000   494. 555 + ____ = 1,000

495. 876 + ____ = 1,000   496. 265 + ____ = 1,000

497. 340 + ____ = 1,000   498. 349 + ____ = 1,000

499. 519 + ____ = 1,000   500. 204 + ____ = 1,000

501. 278 + ____ = 1,000   502. 860 + ____ = 1,000

503. 259 + ____ = 1,000   504. 205 + ____ = 1,000

505. 274 + ____ = 1,000   506. 714 + ____ = 1,000

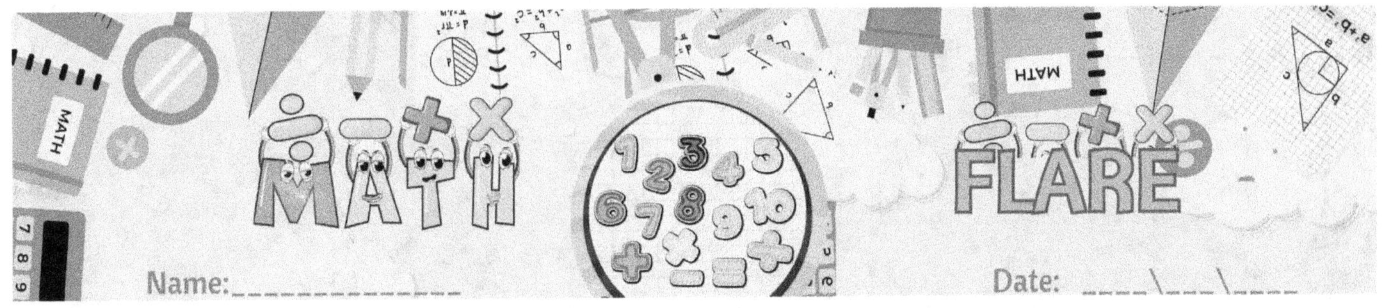

507. 526 + ____ = 1,000

508. 50 + ____ = 1,000

509. 917 + ____ = 1,000

510. 69 + ____ = 1,000

511. 312 + ____ = 1,000

512. 431 + ____ = 1,000

513. 639 + ____ = 1,000

514. 30 + ____ = 1,000

515. 242 + ____ = 1,000

516. 931 + ____ = 1,000

517. 697 + ____ = 1,000

518. 196 + ____ = 1,000

519. 970 + ____ = 1,000

520. 657 + ____ = 1,000

521. 136 + ____ = 1,000

522. 787 + ____ = 1,000

523. 56 + ____ = 1,000

524. 269 + ____ = 1,000

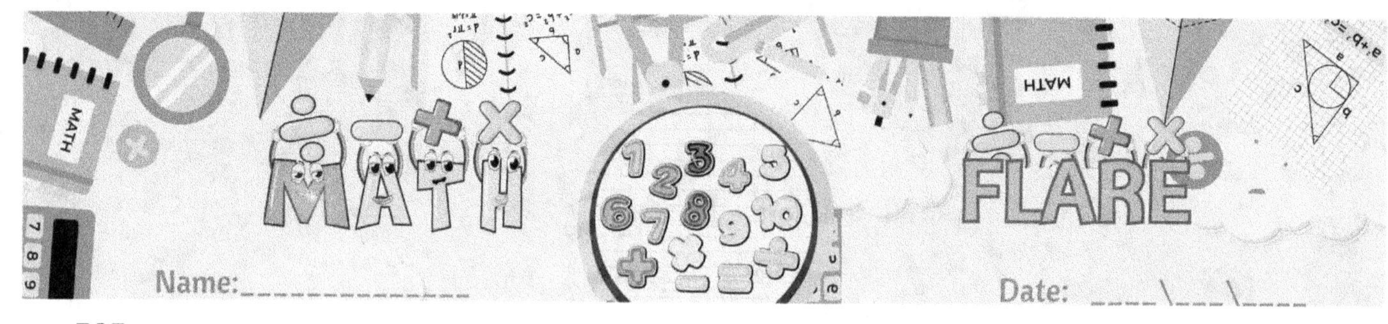

525. 396 + ____ = 1,000

526. 859 + ____ = 1,000

527. 938 + ____ = 1,000

528. 846 + ____ = 1,000

529. 658 + ____ = 1,000

530. 249 + ____ = 1,000

531. 928 + ____ = 1,000

532. 466 + ____ = 1,000

533. 131 + ____ = 1,000

534. 974 + ____ = 1,000

535. 664 + ____ = 1,000

536. 241 + ____ = 1,000

537. 408 + ____ = 1,000

538. 13 + ____ = 1,000

539. 206 + ____ = 1,000

540. 91 + ____ = 1,000

Addition (3 Addends)

Find the sum.

541.
```
   191
   584
 + 693
______
```

542.
```
   545
   512
 + 496
______
```

543.
```
   486
   717
 + 892
______
```

544.
```
   289
   640
 + 349
______
```

545.
```
   358
   773
 + 968
______
```

546.
```
   924
   551
 + 428
______
```

547.
```
   362
   734
 + 704
______
```

548.
```
   985
   231
 + 585
______
```

549.
```
   599
   541
 + 624
______
```

550.
```
   759
   631
 + 627
______
```

551.
```
   605
   185
 + 817
______
```

552.
```
   963
   407
 + 645
______
```

553.
```
   211
   425
 + 729
______
```

554.
```
   833
   689
 + 203
______
```

555.
```
   762
   275
 + 428
______
```

556.
```
   168
   382
 + 441
______
```

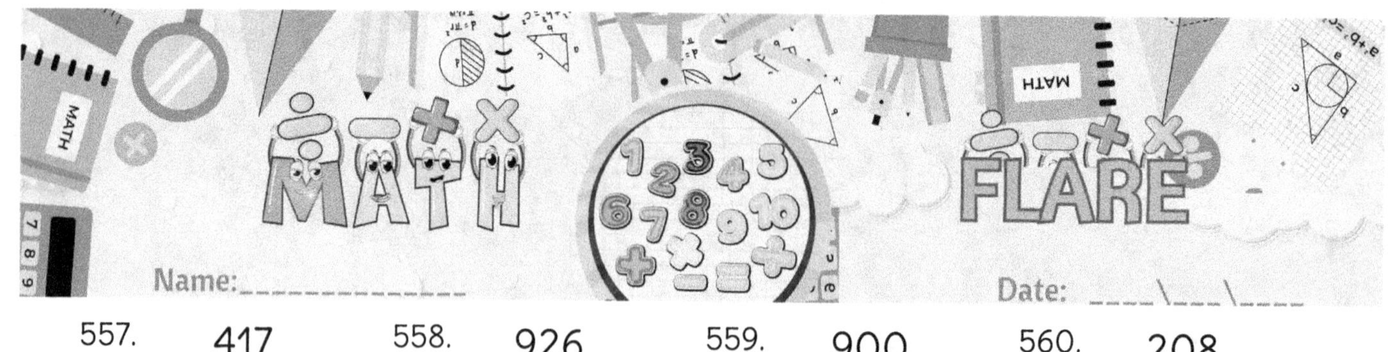

557. 417 386 + 439	558. 926 188 + 100	559. 900 206 + 453	560. 208 945 + 970
561. 871 726 + 186	562. 365 683 + 555	563. 531 394 + 466	564. 423 813 + 226
565. 699 527 + 145	566. 601 323 + 955	567. 257 531 + 259	568. 282 441 + 345
569. 289 678 + 996	570. 816 164 + 302	571. 292 103 + 479	572. 757 961 + 962

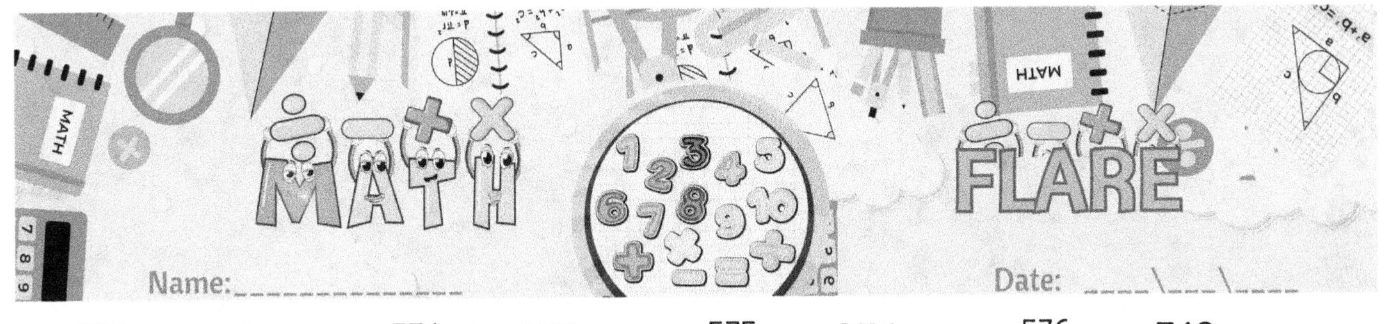

573. 117 497 + 591	574. 872 636 + 987	575. 974 994 + 572	576. 312 327 + 660
577. 955 398 + 882	578. 497 950 + 514	579. 812 689 + 385	580. 840 176 + 105
581. 558 714 + 330	582. 264 230 + 810	583. 747 941 + 565	584. 182 585 + 825
585. 464 383 + 895	586. 271 307 + 447	587. 772 975 + 450	588. 436 861 + 764

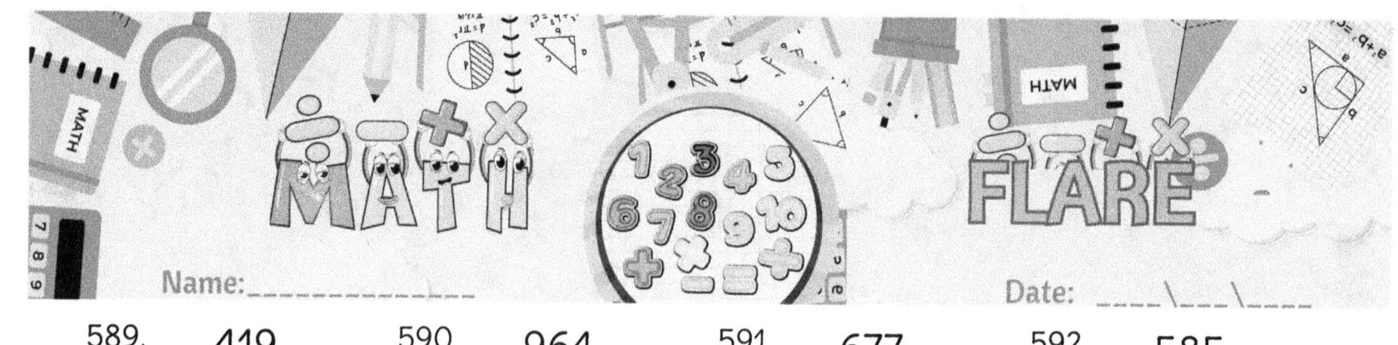

| 589. | 419
794
+ 151 | 590. | 964
944
+ 372 | 591. | 677
276
+ 421 | 592. | 585
414
+ 921 |

| 593. | 757
810
+ 863 | 594. | 761
565
+ 386 | 595. | 195
873
+ 813 | 596. | 156
133
+ 667 |

| 597. | 619
641
+ 482 | 598. | 937
168
+ 200 | 599. | 654
222
+ 852 | 600. | 565
844
+ 436 |

| 601. | 759
782
+ 995 | 602. | 293
504
+ 409 | 603. | 504
878
+ 968 | 604. | 973
513
+ 496 |

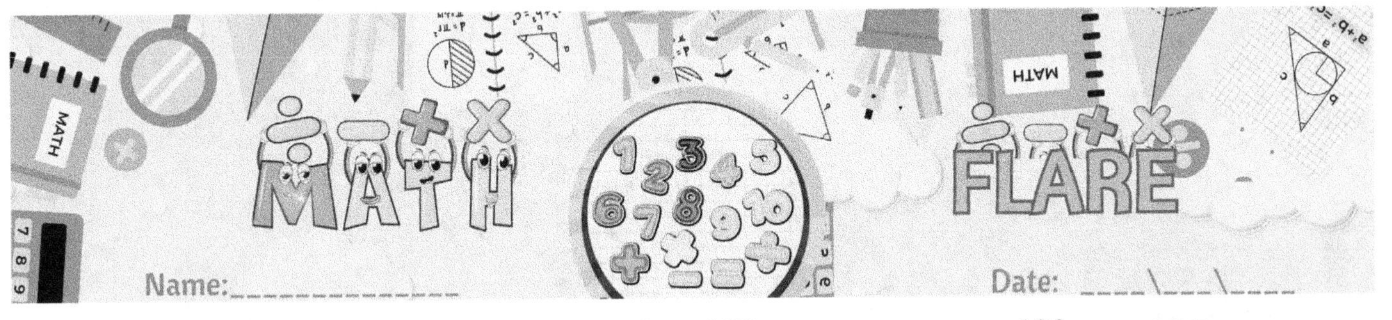

605. 582 110 + 511	606. 165 341 + 987	607. 951 363 + 761	608. 483 445 + 403
609. 890 739 + 207	610. 322 930 + 292	611. 169 292 + 965	612. 528 102 + 782
613. 389 901 + 470	614. 503 651 + 254	615. 698 645 + 228	616. 985 455 + 158
617. 688 590 + 880	618. 865 613 + 582	619. 674 376 + 437	620. 692 403 + 764

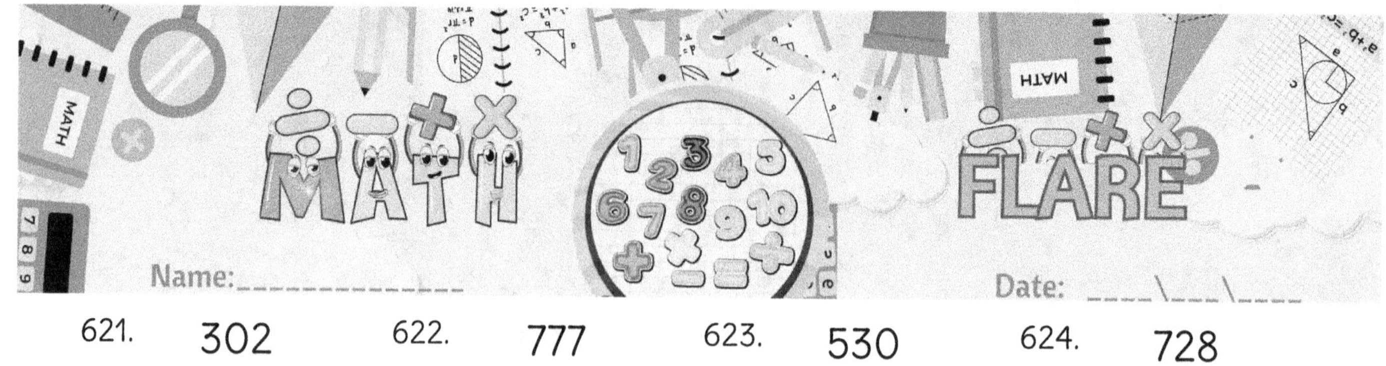

621. 302 283 + 947	622. 777 904 + 321	623. 530 155 + 108	624. 728 774 + 440
625. 617 547 + 710	626. 607 785 + 800	627. 275 904 + 383	628. 149 633 + 441
629. 410 303 + 677	630. 483 853 + 726	631. 445 696 + 598	632. 705 301 + 469
633. 306 920 + 739	634. 906 554 + 400	635. 150 959 + 814	636. 541 348 + 166

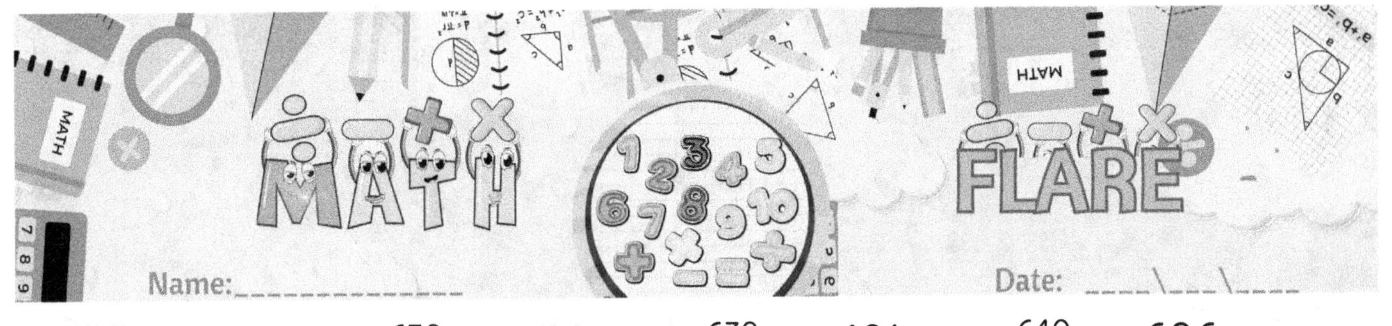

637.　871　167　+ 590

638.　636　517　+ 498

639.　481　253　+ 649

640.　606　467　+ 701

641.　643　147　+ 301

642.　381　382　+ 178

643.　840　911　+ 346

644.　341　401　+ 864

645.　160　368　+ 449

646.　982　998　+ 672

647.　625　869　+ 954

648.　611　612　+ 785

649.　236　809　+ 279

650.　201　324　+ 148

651.　819　699　+ 553

652.　138　362　+ 507

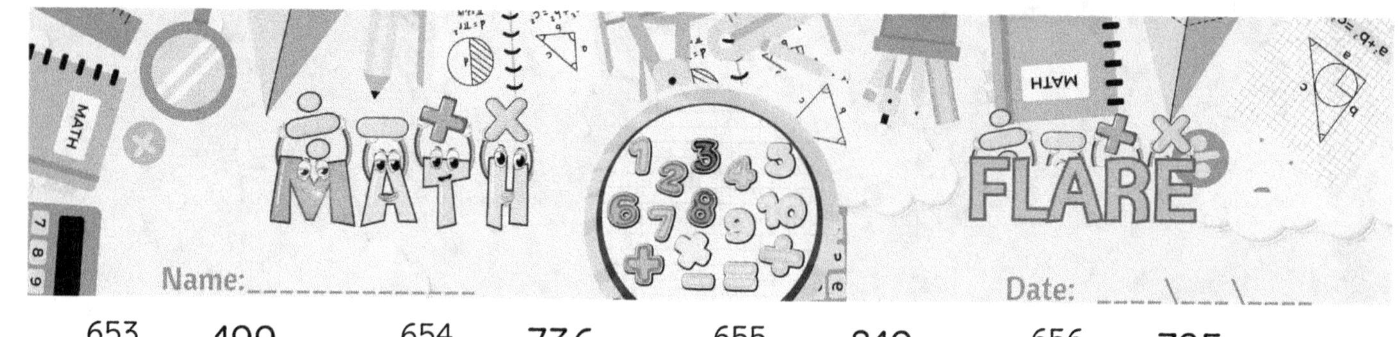

653. 199 768 + 677	654. 736 699 + 435	655. 819 630 + 766	656. 725 576 + 249
657. 148 498 + 254	658. 976 980 + 597	659. 746 132 + 535	660. 515 245 + 573
661. 898 740 + 688	662. 299 521 + 701	663. 411 122 + 106	664. 941 883 + 329
665. 994 888 + 269	666. 619 791 + 981	667. 120 510 + 333	668. 130 152 + 825

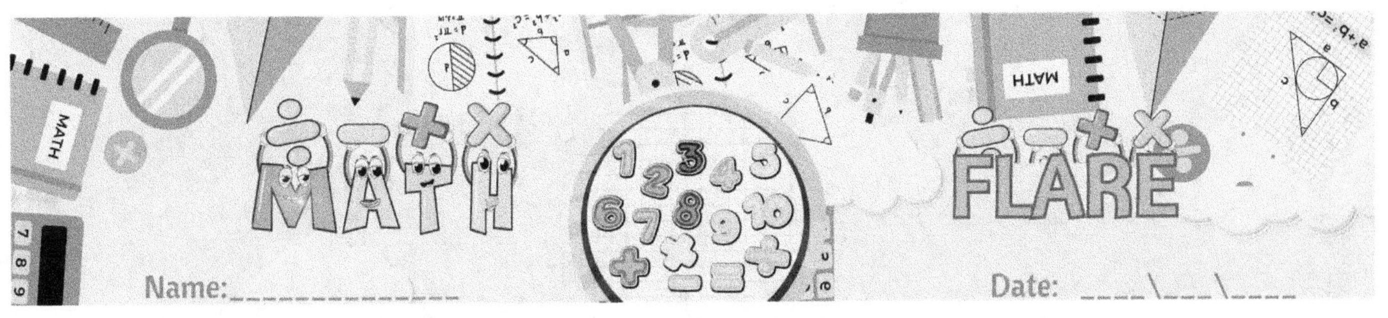

669.
$$\begin{array}{r} 892 \\ 842 \\ +\ 718 \\ \hline \end{array}$$

670.
$$\begin{array}{r} 955 \\ 391 \\ +\ 330 \\ \hline \end{array}$$

671.
$$\begin{array}{r} 972 \\ 684 \\ +\ 623 \\ \hline \end{array}$$

672.
$$\begin{array}{r} 205 \\ 837 \\ +\ 958 \\ \hline \end{array}$$

673.
$$\begin{array}{r} 747 \\ 620 \\ +\ 208 \\ \hline \end{array}$$

674.
$$\begin{array}{r} 165 \\ 414 \\ +\ 554 \\ \hline \end{array}$$

675.
$$\begin{array}{r} 244 \\ 206 \\ +\ 614 \\ \hline \end{array}$$

676.
$$\begin{array}{r} 924 \\ 981 \\ +\ 192 \\ \hline \end{array}$$

677.
$$\begin{array}{r} 427 \\ 226 \\ +\ 340 \\ \hline \end{array}$$

678.
$$\begin{array}{r} 553 \\ 495 \\ +\ 734 \\ \hline \end{array}$$

679.
$$\begin{array}{r} 340 \\ 869 \\ +\ 687 \\ \hline \end{array}$$

680.
$$\begin{array}{r} 861 \\ 405 \\ +\ 678 \\ \hline \end{array}$$

681.
$$\begin{array}{r} 981 \\ 455 \\ +\ 730 \\ \hline \end{array}$$

682.
$$\begin{array}{r} 775 \\ 968 \\ +\ 299 \\ \hline \end{array}$$

683.
$$\begin{array}{r} 705 \\ 889 \\ +\ 151 \\ \hline \end{array}$$

684.
$$\begin{array}{r} 310 \\ 872 \\ +\ 272 \\ \hline \end{array}$$

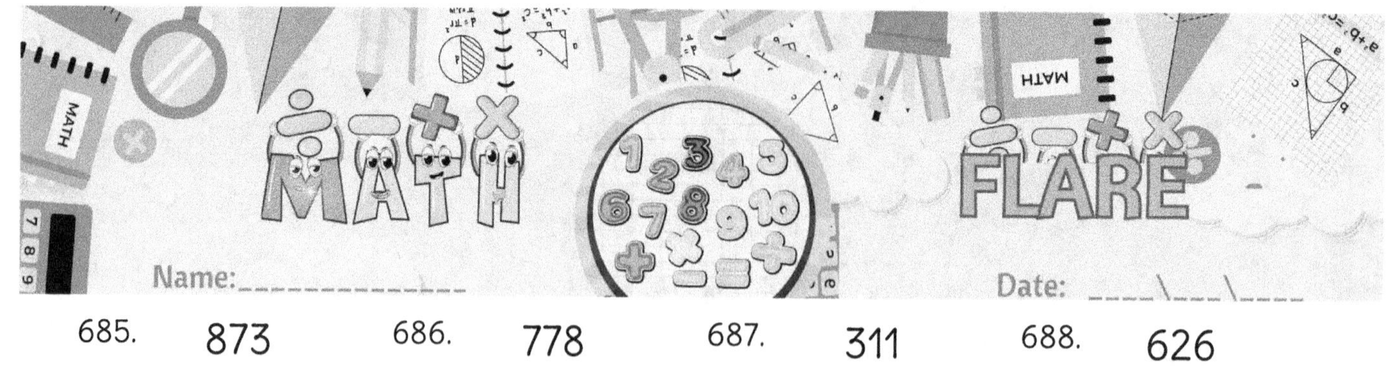

685. 873
      954
    + 197
    ______

686. 778
      885
    + 945
    ______

687. 311
      968
    + 861
    ______

688. 626
      628
    + 265
    ______

689. 989
      519
    + 289
    ______

690. 889
      864
    + 967
    ______

691. 371
      884
    + 315
    ______

692. 530
      183
    + 958
    ______

693. 822
      468
    + 237
    ______

694. 415
      319
    + 191
    ______

695. 140
      217
    + 354
    ______

696. 168
      679
    + 540
    ______

697. 637
      561
    + 983
    ______

698. 741
      650
    + 437
    ______

699. 816
      455
    + 826
    ______

700. 565
      784
    + 549
    ______

41

Name: _______________________   Date: ____ \ ____ \ ____

701.	702.	703.	704.

701.
$$110$$
$$815$$
$$+\ 126$$

702.
$$183$$
$$938$$
$$+\ 987$$

703.
$$956$$
$$443$$
$$+\ 871$$

704.
$$238$$
$$955$$
$$+\ 517$$

705.
$$809$$
$$895$$
$$+\ 749$$

706.
$$770$$
$$586$$
$$+\ 510$$

707.
$$910$$
$$921$$
$$+\ 839$$

708.
$$748$$
$$352$$
$$+\ 403$$

709.
$$983$$
$$629$$
$$+\ 334$$

710.
$$877$$
$$713$$
$$+\ 726$$

711.
$$231$$
$$357$$
$$+\ 683$$

712.
$$687$$
$$405$$
$$+\ 503$$

713.
$$165$$
$$956$$
$$+\ 278$$

714.
$$366$$
$$211$$
$$+\ 336$$

715.
$$668$$
$$499$$
$$+\ 605$$

716.
$$566$$
$$931$$
$$+\ 754$$

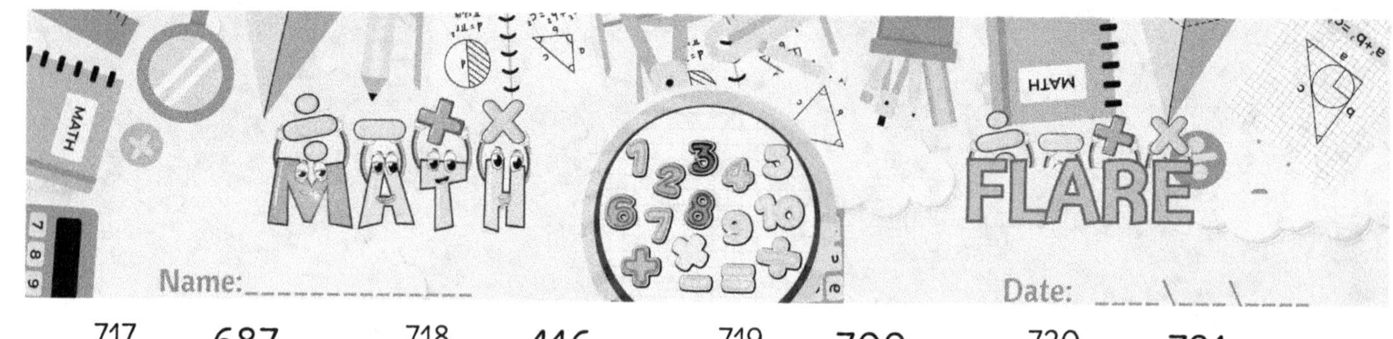

717. 687 146 + 868	718. 416 654 + 863	719. 709 362 + 563	720. 721 199 + 409
721. 753 179 + 729	722. 245 107 + 698	723. 833 222 + 591	724. 346 704 + 629
725. 332 644 + 809	726. 603 180 + 852	727. 798 517 + 696	728. 579 290 + 667
729. 857 814 + 702	730. 819 977 + 143	731. 939 443 + 857	732. 868 613 + 133

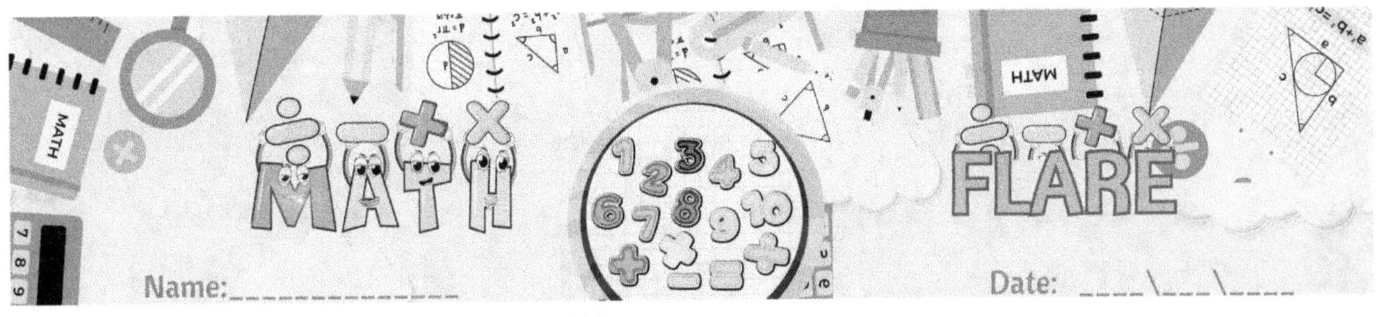

Multiple Operations: Addition Subtraction

Find the sum.

733. 855 490 - 432 - 218	734. 989 - 293 379 - 265	735. 790 - 152 709 - 284
736. 869 - 353 - 271 395	737. 563 - 528 - 35 970	738. 757 - 243 742 - 377
739. 601 - 144 - 120 828	740. 802 - 178 325 - 394	741. 857 - 326 691 - 478
742. 802 449 - 148 - 277	743. 657 - 487 - 108 528	744. 921 - 126 - 310 472

745.	746.	747.
849 925 - 385 - 478	954 - 140 593 - 262	874 209 - 166 - 495

748.	749.	750.
717 551 - 462 - 262	939 120 - 425 - 193	957 - 355 788 - 389

751.	752.	753.
929 883 - 426 - 369	638 313 - 456 - 122	833 679 - 164 - 390

754.	755.	756.
792 468 - 439 - 367	979 367 - 154 - 298	657 307 - 109 - 433

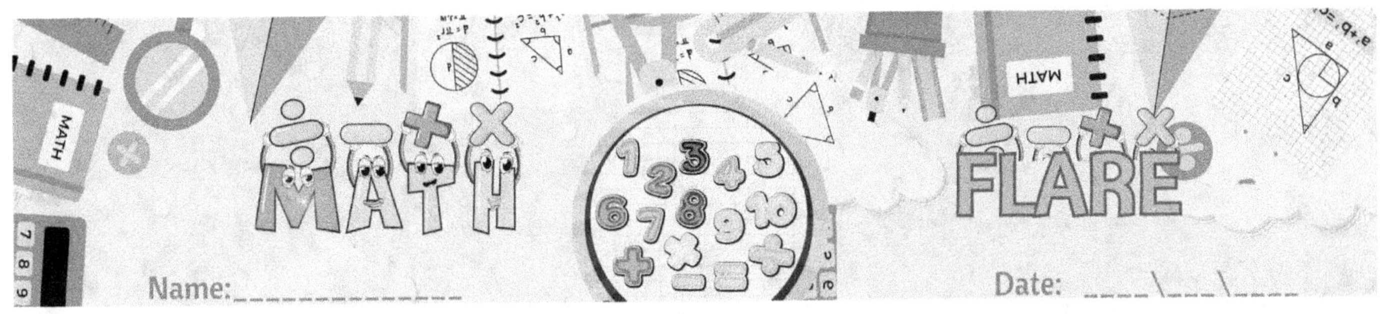

757.   573
     785
-   374
-   461
____
	758. 699
	- 217
	     557
	- 143
	_______
		759. 617
		     992
		- 548
		- 113
		_______

760.   713
     953
-   173
-   317
____
	761. 697
	- 140
	- 211
	     756
	_______
		762. 710
		- 172
		     838
		- 305
		_______

763.   670
-   158
-   204
     648
____
	764. 750
	- 245
	- 263
	     652
	_______
		765. 931
		- 543
		     590
		- 296
		_______

766.   831
-   544
     751
-   266
____
	767. 610
	     142
	- 321
	- 281
	_______
		768. 735
		     752
		- 204
		- 102
		_______

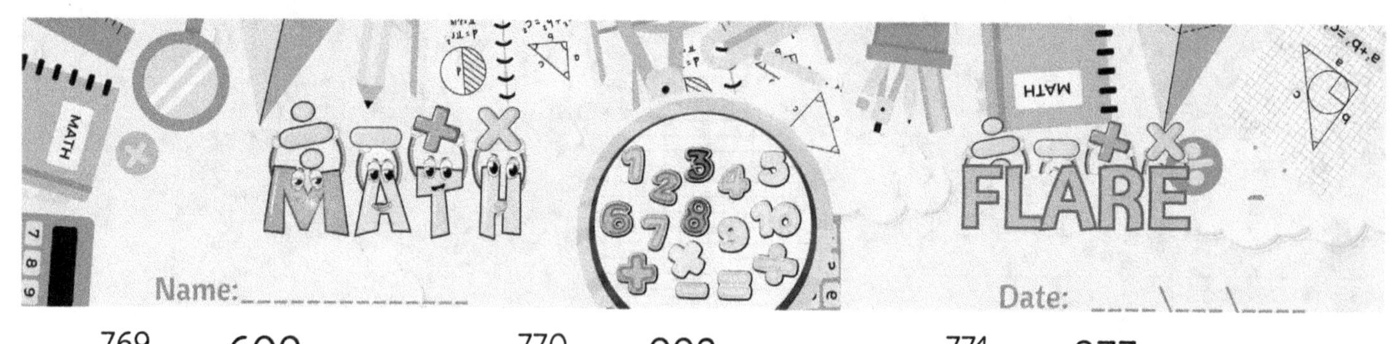

769.   609
      673
− 150
− 168
 	
———
	770. 992
	− 231
	− 272
	    904
	
	———
		771. 973
		     238
		− 340
		− 192
		
		———

772.   552
     908
− 392
− 473
 	
———
	773. 815
	− 272
	    262
	− 270
	
	———
		774. 731
		     754
		− 486
		− 253
		
		———

775.   714
− 495
− 171
    379
 	
———
	776. 850
	     344
	− 119
	− 345
	
	———
		777. 953
		     321
		− 314
		− 464
		
		———

778.   644
− 212
    668
− 350
 	
———
	779. 820
	− 392
	    544
	− 312
	
	———
		780. 754
		     567
		− 262
		− 207
		
		———

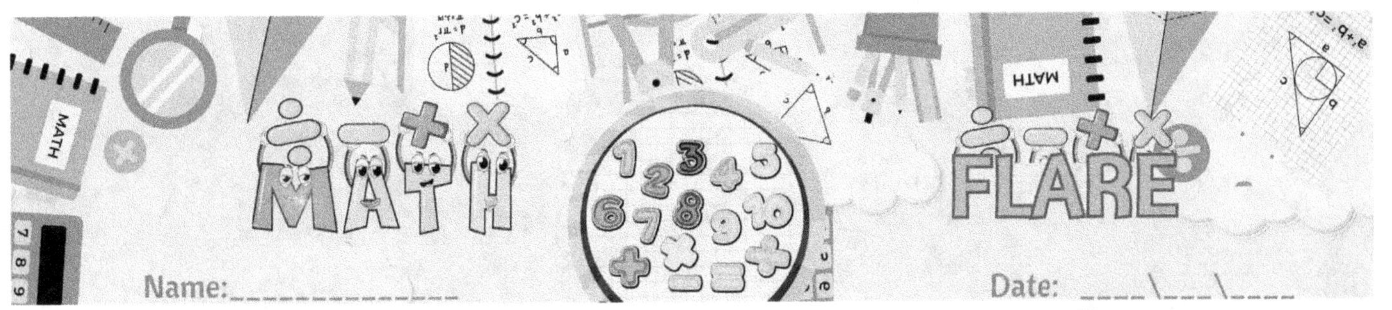

781.
```
    728
  - 398
    962
  - 113
  ______
```

782.
```
    794
  - 483
  - 227
    466
  ______
```

783.
```
    900
    793
  - 453
  - 147
  ______
```

784.
```
    864
  - 132
    301
  - 401
  ______
```

785.
```
    598
    990
  - 238
  - 443
  ______
```

786.
```
    739
    854
  - 377
  - 252
  ______
```

787.
```
    887
    661
  - 448
  - 438
  ______
```

788.
```
    653
  - 273
  - 349
    862
  ______
```

789.
```
    782
    419
  - 510
  - 102
  ______
```

790.
```
    690
    113
  - 100
  - 120
  ______
```

791.
```
    839
    161
  - 114
  - 298
  ______
```

792.
```
    758
    573
  - 485
  - 338
  ______
```

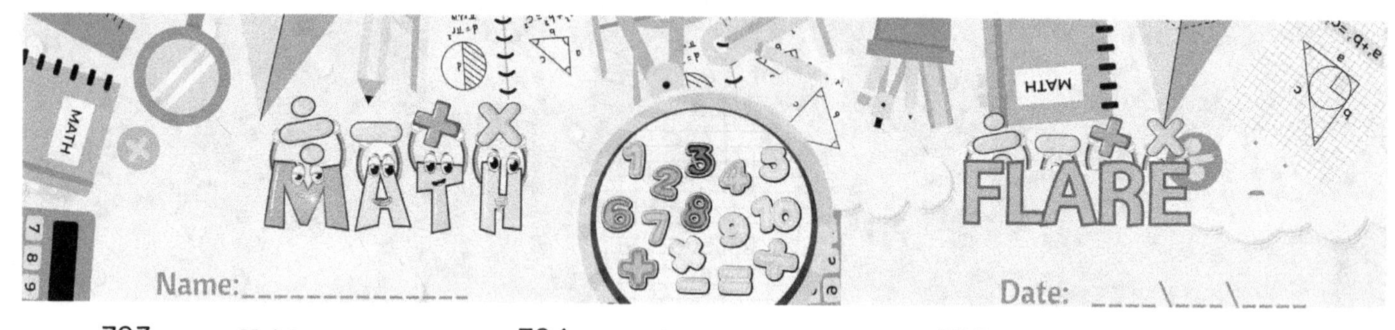

793.   741
− 470
   426
− 309
	794. 644
	− 369
	− 243
	   604
		795. 569
		   656
		− 225
		− 514

796.   584
− 481
− 100
   454
	797. 947
	   943
	− 364
	− 254
		798. 621
		− 198
		− 215
		   185

799.   994
   335
− 152
− 259
	800. 912
	   259
	− 493
	− 201
		801. 894
		− 210
		   394
		− 283

802.   559
− 289
− 208
   926
	803. 792
	− 258
	− 517
	   725
		804. 881
		   171
		− 535
		− 432

805.
```
    952
    674
  - 350
  - 337
  ______

```

806.
```
    972
  - 331
    433
  - 193
  ______

```

807.
```
    760
    340
  - 314
  - 527
  ______

```

808.
```
    765
  - 307
    778
  - 490
  ______

```

809.
```
    884
    147
  - 169
  - 474
  ______

```

810.
```
    784
    789
  - 266
  - 308
  ______

```

811.
```
    685
    702
  - 461
  - 463
  ______

```

812.
```
    665
  - 397
  - 160
    918
  ______

```

813.
```
    682
  - 244
  - 255
    251
  ______

```

814.
```
    828
    411
  - 228
  - 213
  ______

```

815.
```
    943
    206
  - 523
  - 440
  ______

```

816.
```
    974
  - 408
    493
  - 135
  ______

```

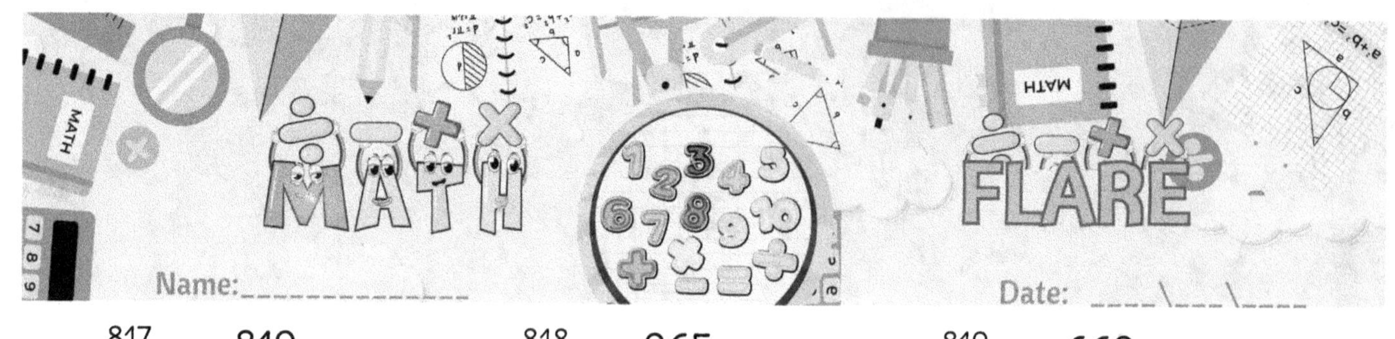

817. 819
  182
− 528
− 355
	818. 965
	− 160
	  347
	− 157
		819. 669
		− 141
		− 196
		  342

820. 868
− 352
  954
− 463
	821. 958
	− 355
	  689
	− 172
		822. 549
		− 363
		  323
		− 263

823. 894
  912
− 531
− 281
	824. 921
	− 376
	− 332
	  655
		825. 653
		  753
		− 194
		− 174

826. 868
  708
− 543
− 172
	827. 569
	− 249
	− 299
	  575
		828. 603
		− 107
		  588
		− 240

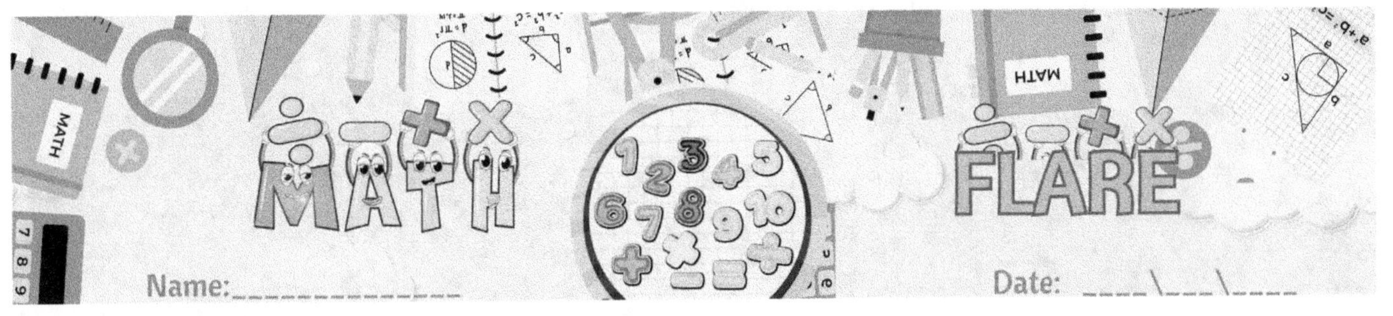

829. 625
− 159
− 411
  437
______
	830. 562
	  349
	− 134
	− 106
	______
		831. 929
		− 349
		− 512
		  119
		______

832. 627
  884
− 235
− 394
______
	833. 806
	  646
	− 116
	− 542
	______
		834. 707
		− 452
		− 115
		  308
		______

835. 811
  544
− 151
− 401
______
	836. 857
	  747
	− 224
	− 437
	______
		837. 711
		− 390
		  310
		− 412
		______

838. 894
− 165
− 364
  958
______
	839. 842
	− 187
	  390
	− 169
	______
		840. 891
		  967
		− 543
		− 178
		______

841.
```
   563
 - 211
 - 342
   562
_______
```

842.
```
   990
 - 351
 - 531
   446
_______
```

843.
```
   563
 - 377
 - 168
   583
_______
```

844.
```
   622
   466
 - 248
 - 155
_______
```

845.
```
   674
 - 175
 - 364
   575
_______
```

846.
```
   836
 - 373
   900
 - 291
_______
```

847.
```
   558
 - 137
 - 207
   241
_______
```

848.
```
   757
   949
 - 312
 - 378
_______
```

849.
```
   777
   945
 - 387
 - 296
_______
```

850.
```
   893
 - 442
   793
 - 460
_______
```

851.
```
   858
   863
 - 397
 - 166
_______
```

852.
```
   708
   145
 - 455
 - 172
_______
```

Name:________________   Date: _______________

853.	854.	855.

853.
```
   938
   278
 - 495
 - 366
 ______
```

854.
```
   685
   512
 - 341
 - 290
 ______
```

855.
```
   710
   578
 - 322
 - 503
 ______
```

856.
```
   651
   822
 - 515
 - 140
 ______
```

857.
```
   614
   257
 - 113
 - 200
 ______
```

858.
```
   895
 - 502
   425
 - 331
 ______
```

859.
```
   727
 - 487
 - 218
   810
 ______
```

860.
```
   975
   766
 - 132
 - 536
 ______
```

861.
```
   681
 - 140
 - 229
   336
 ______
```

862.
```
   578
   890
 - 241
 - 121
 ______
```

863.
```
   731
 - 196
 - 134
   308
 ______
```

864.
```
   670
   886
 - 358
 - 497
 ______
```

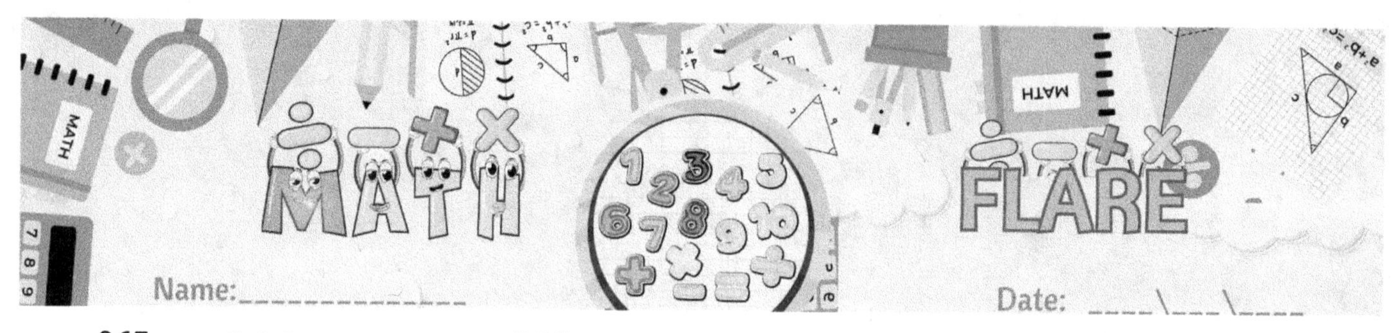

865.
```
   966
 - 357
   102
 - 179
 ______
```

866.
```
   558
   609
 - 312
 - 536
 ______
```

867.
```
   926
   426
 - 188
 - 299
 ______
```

868.
```
   827
 - 435
 - 239
   655
 ______
```

869.
```
   755
 - 335
 - 293
   221
 ______
```

870.
```
   779
 - 397
 - 106
   340
 ______
```

871.
```
   937
   983
 - 469
 - 349
 ______
```

872.
```
   917
 - 158
   322
 - 335
 ______
```

873.
```
   678
   961
 - 489
 - 268
 ______
```

874.
```
   882
 - 502
 - 366
   753
 ______
```

875.
```
   827
 - 244
 - 291
   732
 ______
```

876.
```
   856
 - 492
 - 214
   691
 ______
```

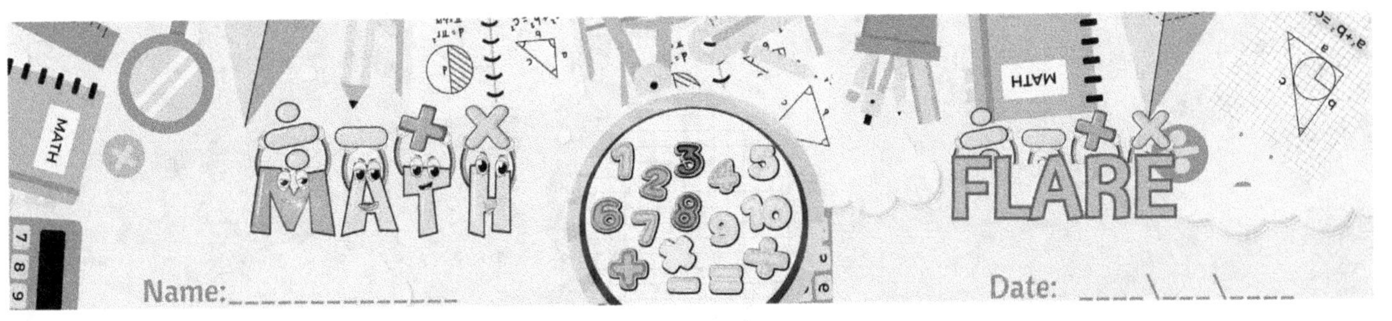

877.	878.	879.
881	671	795
514	− 297	− 431
− 447	436	385
− 434	− 218	− 117

880.	881.	882.
885	601	946
925	− 403	− 146
− 169	− 115	− 495
− 418	693	606

883.	884.	885.
808	655	796
889	− 244	− 173
− 332	− 282	− 468
− 184	990	419

886.	887.	888.
709	812	809
552	− 370	− 508
− 213	− 383	− 297
− 481	102	730

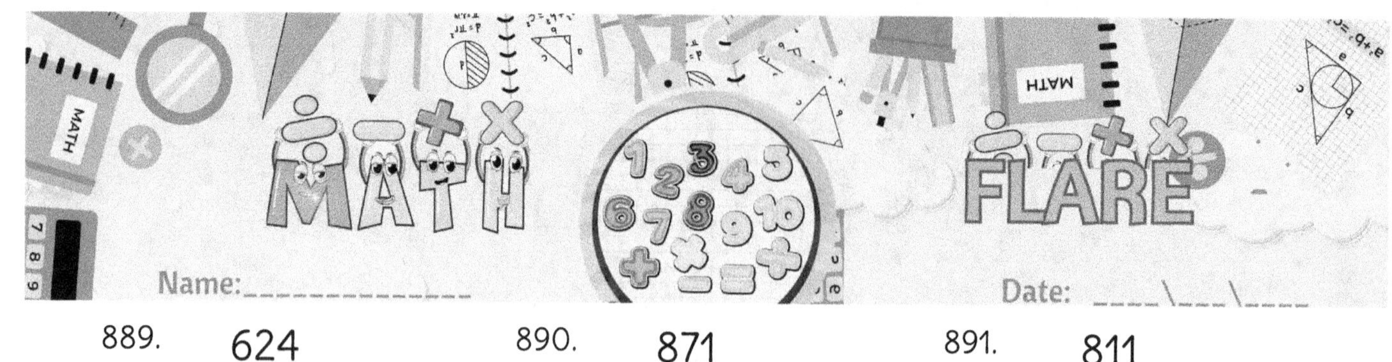

889. 624 746 − 364 − 103	890. 871 795 − 449 − 385	891. 811 − 194 − 175 454
892. 964 − 183 − 112 303	893. 617 395 − 320 − 362	894. 593 819 − 257 − 375
895. 739 − 238 168 − 226	896. 673 888 − 543 − 400	897. 953 − 467 − 107 564
898. 879 − 359 345 − 449	899. 723 266 − 447 − 164	900. 699 871 − 517 − 278

901.   807
  − 370
  − 387
    325
	902. 737
	  − 278
	    641
	  − 265
		903. 714
		    977
		  − 363
		  − 283

904.   863
  − 322
  − 258
    735
	905. 650
	  − 325
	  − 212
	    193
		906. 623
		  − 330
		  − 195
		    616

907.   573
  − 421
    276
  − 400
	908. 560
	    284
	  − 225
	  − 354
		909. 720
		  − 405
		    737
		  − 403

910.   559
    760
  − 212
  − 325
	911. 646
	  − 393
	  − 122
	    782
		912. 996
		    877
		  − 135
		  − 501

913.   921
    - 129
     929
    - 474
	914. 711
	    - 470
	    - 132
	     154
		915. 597
		     349
		    - 187
		    - 416

916.   639
    - 409
     408
    - 173
	917. 862
	    - 108
	     126
	    - 108
		918. 904
		    - 407
		     714
		    - 320

919.   662
    - 548
    - 113
     563
	920. 712
	     761
	    - 362
	    - 185
		921. 835
		    - 237
		    - 139
		     964

922.   676
    - 300
    - 156
     599
	923. 750
	    - 391
	    - 247
	     771
		924. 791
		     591
		    - 235
		    - 338

ANSWERS

Page 1: Addition with Regrouping

1. 1,651	2. 1,343	3. 1,310	4. 1,611	5. 1,830	6. 1,110
7. 1,531	8. 1,120	9. 1,127	10. 1,241	11. 1,960	12. 1,244
13. 1,376	14. 1,112	15. 1,450	16. 1,113	17. 1,210	18. 1,425
19. 1,130	20. 1,961	21. 1,450	22. 1,710	23. 1,131	24. 1,121
25. 1,513	26. 1,510	27. 1,230	28. 1,740	29. 1,110	30. 1,575
31. 1,323	32. 1,350	33. 1,130	34. 1,340	35. 1,412	36. 1,413
37. 1,270	38. 1,550	39. 1,212	40. 1,410	41. 1,172	42. 1,724
43. 1,112	44. 1,234	45. 1,320	46. 1,121	47. 1,221	48. 1,110
49. 1,410	50. 1,212	51. 1,312	52. 1,342	53. 1,310	54. 1,310
55. 1,513	56. 1,320	57. 1,123	58. 1,111	59. 1,410	60. 1,110
61. 1,363	62. 1,413	63. 1,443	64. 1,310	65. 1,535	66. 1,273
67. 1,110	68. 1,413	69. 1,524	70. 1,433	71. 1,581	72. 1,161
73. 1,510	74. 1,631	75. 1,210	76. 1,520	77. 1,130	78. 1,312
79. 1,242	80. 1,124	81. 1,220	82. 1,111	83. 1,212	84. 1,212
85. 1,140	86. 1,230	87. 1,226	88. 1,330	89. 1,450	90. 1,314
91. 1,220	92. 1,130	93. 1,442	94. 1,533	95. 1,930	96. 1,244
97. 1,116	98. 1,110	99. 1,331	100. 1,760	101. 1,530	102. 1,540
103. 1,230	104. 1,710	105. 1,130	106. 1,510	107. 1,113	108. 1,416

109. 1,250   110. 1,191   111. 1,131   112. 1,172   113. 1,391   114. 1,210

115. 1,133   116. 1,212   117. 1,430   118. 1,110   119. 1,242   120. 1,560

121. 1,110   122. 1,121   123. 1,125   124. 1,110   125. 1,263   126. 1,111

127. 1,231   128. 1,311   129. 1,120   130. 1,126   131. 1,110   132. 1,246

133. 1,412   134. 1,222   135. 1,340   136. 1,520   137. 1,214   138. 1,143

139. 1,120   140. 1,114   141. 1,250   142. 1,330   143. 1,183   144. 1,641

145. 1,210   146. 1,610   147. 1,330   148. 1,511   149. 1,710   150. 1,615

151. 1,261   152. 1,210   153. 1,221   154. 1,313   155. 1,110   156. 1,610

Page 9: Subtraction with Regrouping

157. 89   158. 188   159. 187   160. 269   161. 69   162. 283

163. 167   164. 389   165. 89   166. 81   167. 16   168. 39

169. 559   170. 189   171. 684   172. 21   173. 189   174. 78

175. 75   176. 139   177. 359   178. 273   179. 187   180. 465

181. 45   182. 223   183. 178   184. 469   185. 148   186. 167

187. 189   188. 89   189. 69   190. 89   191. 288   192. 459

193. 88   194. 189   195. 89   196. 82   197. 76   198. 669

199. 89   200. 36   201. 87   202. 189   203. 57   204. 89

205. 183   206. 137   207. 89   208. 89   209. 78   210. 169

211. 89   212. 76   213. 79   214. 89   215. 85   216. 156

217. 587   218. 185   219. 419   220. 169   221. 483   222. 359

223. 87   224. 87   225. 258   226. 236   227. 179   228. 69

229. 184	230. 58	231. 89	232. 39	233. 276	234. 574
235. 85	236. 57	237. 84	238. 171	239. 68	240. 271
241. 287	242. 82	243. 682	244. 67	245. 776	246. 85
247. 47	248. 76	249. 188	250. 47	251. 389	252. 782
253. 159	254. 81	255. 88	256. 74	257. 188	258. 429
259. 286	260. 88	261. 88	262. 75	263. 489	264. 85
265. 188	266. 57	267. 167	268. 48	269. 37	270. 156
271. 29	272. 477	273. 149	274. 38	275. 174	276. 228
277. 219	278. 86	279. 384	280. 169	281. 667	282. 187
283. 646	284. 288				

Page 17: Addition Unknown Number

285. 110	286. 113	287. 156	288. 53	289. 56	290. 99
291. 110	292. 141	293. 59	294. 111	295. 28	296. 126
297. 120	298. 8	299. 99	300. 110	301. 93	302. 8
303. 137	304. 72	305. 32	306. 115	307. 112	308. 16
309. 99	310. 132	311. 140	312. 120	313. 99	314. 4
315. 51	316. 21	317. 123	318. 75	319. 87	320. 155
321. 144	322. 45	323. 34	324. 78	325. 144	326. 16
327. 7	328. 120	329. 70	330. 65	331. 25	332. 99
333. 130	334. 81	335. 67	336. 25	337. 97	338. 31
339. 12	340. 160	341. 18	342. 39	343. 113	344. 99

345. 7   346. 26   347. 86   348. 98   349. 123   350. 88

351. 120   352. 49   353. 82   354. 85   355. 63   356. 44

357. 122   358. 29   359. 160   360. 110   361. 7   362. 67

363. 61   364. 62   365. 98   366. 29   367. 124   368. 58

369. 37   370. 153   371. 55   372. 113   373. 23   374. 146

375. 131   376. 31   377. 113   378. 27   379. 3   380. 99

381. 122   382. 66   383. 136   384. 150   385. 77   386. 122

Page 23: Subtraction: Unknown Number

387. 46   388. 84   389. 5   390. 3   391. 14   392. 20   393. 17

394. 92   395. 9   396. 43   397. 10   398. 12   399. 41   400. 96

401. 99   402. 56   403. 62   404. 11   405. 72   406. 79   407. 26

408. 1   409. 59   410. 25   411. 78   412. 16   413. 89   414. 94

415. 54   416. 40   417. 1   418. 49   419. 51   420. 52   421. 3

422. 53   423. 73   424. 40   425. 15   426. 21   427. 54   428. 62

429. 27   430. 65   431. 25   432. 23   433. 41   434. 11   435. 17

436. 46   437. 18   438. 43   439. 57   440. 67   441. 4   442. 26

443. 18   444. 94   445. 43   446. 21   447. 23   448. 64   449. 2

450. 87   451. 44   452. 84   453. 44   454. 51   455. 50   456. 39

457. 65   458. 12   459. 10   460. 59   461. 50   462. 18   463. 11

464. 18   465. 8   466. 19   467. 98   468. 30   469. 11   470. 51

471. 51   472. 27   473. 95   474. 22   475. 11   476. 35   477. 0

478. 20   479. 2   480. 80   481. 18   482. 65   483. 32   484. 3

485. 57   486. 38   487. 72   488. 75   489. 44   490. 78

Make 1000

491. 461   492. 903   493. 797   494. 445   495. 124   496. 735

497. 660   498. 651   499. 481   500. 796   501. 722   502. 140

503. 741   504. 795   505. 726   506. 286   507. 474   508. 950

509. 83   510. 931   511. 688   512. 569   513. 361   514. 970

515. 758   516. 69   517. 303   518. 804   519. 30   520. 343

521. 864   522. 213   523. 944   524. 731   525. 604   526. 141

527. 62   528. 154   529. 342   530. 751   531. 72   532. 534

533. 869   534. 26   535. 336   536. 759   537. 592   538. 987

539. 794   540. 909

Page 32: Addition (3 Addends)

541. 1,468   542. 1,553   543. 2,095   544. 1,278   545. 2,099

546. 1,903   547. 1,800   548. 1,801   549. 1,764   550. 2,017

551. 1,607   552. 2,015   553. 1,365   554. 1,725   555. 1,465

556. 991   557. 1,242   558. 1,214   559. 1,559   560. 2,123

561. 1,783   562. 1,603   563. 1,391   564. 1,462   565. 1,371

566. 1,879   567. 1,047   568. 1,068   569. 1,963   570. 1,282

571. 874   572. 2,680   573. 1,205   574. 2,495   575. 2,540

576. 1,299   577. 2,235   578. 1,961   579. 1,886   580. 1,121

581. 1,602   582. 1,304   583. 2,253   584. 1,592   585. 1,742

586. 1,025   587. 2,197   588. 2,061   589. 1,364   590. 2,280

591. 1,374   592. 1,920   593. 2,430   594. 1,712   595. 1,881

596. 956   597. 1,742   598. 1,305   599. 1,728   600. 1,845

601. 2,536   602. 1,206   603. 2,350   604. 1,982   605. 1,203

606. 1,493   607. 2,075   608. 1,331   609. 1,836   610. 1,544

611. 1,426   612. 1,412   613. 1,760   614. 1,408   615. 1,571

616. 1,598   617. 2,158   618. 2,060   619. 1,487   620. 1,859

621. 1,532   622. 2,002   623. 793   624. 1,942   625. 1,874

626. 2,192   627. 1,562   628. 1,223   629. 1,390   630. 2,062

631. 1,739   632. 1,475   633. 1,965   634. 1,860   635. 1,923

636. 1,055   637. 1,628   638. 1,651   639. 1,383   640. 1,774

641. 1,091   642. 941   643. 2,097   644. 1,606   645. 977

646. 2,652   647. 2,448   648. 2,008   649. 1,324   650. 673

651. 2,071   652. 1,007   653. 1,644   654. 1,870   655. 2,215

656. 1,550   657. 900   658. 2,553   659. 1,413   660. 1,333

661. 2,326   662. 1,521   663. 639   664. 2,153   665. 2,151

666. 2,391   667. 963   668. 1,107   669. 2,452   670. 1,676

671. 2,279   672. 2,000   673. 1,575   674. 1,133   675. 1,064

676. 2,097   677. 993   678. 1,782   679. 1,896   680. 1,944

681. 2,166   682. 2,042   683. 1,745   684. 1,454   685. 2,024

686. 2,608   687. 2,140   688. 1,519   689. 1,797   690. 2,720

691. 1,570   692. 1,671   693. 1,527   694. 925   695. 711

696. 1,387   697. 2,181   698. 1,828   699. 2,097   700. 1,898

701. 1,051   702. 2,108   703. 2,270   704. 1,710   705. 2,453

706. 1,866   707. 2,670   708. 1,503   709. 1,946   710. 2,316

711. 1,271   712. 1,595   713. 1,399   714. 913   715. 1,772

716. 2,251   717. 1,701   718. 1,933   719. 1,634   720. 1,329

721. 1,661   722. 1,050   723. 1,646   724. 1,679   725. 1,785

726. 1,635   727. 2,011   728. 1,536   729. 2,373   730. 1,939

731. 2,239   732. 1,614

Page 44: Multiple Operations: Addition Subtraction

733. 695   734. 810   735. 1,063   736. 640   737. 970

738. 879   739. 1,165   740. 555   741. 744   742. 826

743. 590   744. 957   745. 911   746. 1,145   747. 422

748. 544   749. 441   750. 1,001   751. 1,017   752. 373

753. 958   754. 454   755. 894   756. 422   757. 523

758. 896   759. 948   760. 1,176   761. 1,102   762. 1,071

763. 956   764. 894   765. 682   766. 772   767. 150

768. 1,181   769. 964   770. 1,393   771. 679   772. 595

773. 535   774. 746   775. 427   776. 730   777. 496

778. 750   779. 660   780. 852   781. 1,179   782. 550

783. 1,093	784. 632	785. 907	786. 964	787. 662
788. 893	789. 589	790. 583	791. 588	792. 508
793. 388	794. 636	795. 486	796. 457	797. 1,272
798. 393	799. 918	800. 477	801. 795	802. 988
803. 742	804. 85	805. 939	806. 881	807. 259
808. 746	809. 388	810. 999	811. 463	812. 1,026
813. 434	814. 798	815. 186	816. 924	817. 118
818. 995	819. 674	820. 1,007	821. 1,120	822. 246
823. 994	824. 868	825. 1,038	826. 861	827. 596
828. 844	829. 492	830. 671	831. 187	832. 882
833. 794	834. 448	835. 803	836. 943	837. 219
838. 1,323	839. 876	840. 1,137	841. 572	842. 554
843. 601	844. 685	845. 710	846. 1,072	847. 455
848. 1,016	849. 1,039	850. 784	851. 1,158	852. 226
853. 355	854. 566	855. 463	856. 818	857. 558
858. 487	859. 832	860. 1,073	861. 648	862. 1,106
863. 709	864. 701	865. 532	866. 319	867. 865
868. 808	869. 348	870. 616	871. 1,102	872. 746
873. 882	874. 767	875. 1,024	876. 841	877. 514
878. 592	879. 632	880. 1,223	881. 776	882. 911
883. 1,181	884. 1,119	885. 574	886. 567	887. 161

888. 734   889. 903   890. 832   891. 896   892. 972

893. 330   894. 780   895. 443   896. 618   897. 943

898. 416   899. 378   900. 775   901. 375   902. 835

903. 1,045   904. 1,018   905. 306   906. 714   907. 28

908. 265   909. 649   910. 782   911. 913   912. 1,237

913. 1,247   914. 263   915. 343   916. 465   917. 772

918. 891   919. 564   920. 926   921. 1,423   922. 819

923. 883   924. 809

9 7 9 8 8 6 9 3 7 2 5 5 0